Mark's
Passion Narrative

Reflections on
Christ's Sufferings and Death

Dr. David Ewert

MARK'S PASSION NARRATIVE
REFLECTIONS ON CHRIST'S SUFFERINGS AND DEATH

Copyright 2003, 2017

Published by HeartBeat Productions
Box 633
Abbotsford, BC
Canada V2T 6Z8
email: heartbeatproductions@gmail.com

National Library of Canada cataloguing in Publication Data

Ewert, David. 1922-2010

Mark's Passion Narrative: Reflections on Christ's sufferings and death

Includes index.

ISBN 1-895112-13-3

1. Bible. N.T. Mark—Sermons. 2. Jesus Christ—Passion—Sermons. 3. Sermons. Canadian (English) I. Title.

BS2585.54.E93 2003 252'.62 C2003-910428-1

Scripture Quotations are taken from the New Revised Standard Version

All rights reserved. No portion of this book may be reproduced in any form without the written permission of the publisher.

Printed in Canada

MARK'S PASSION NARRATIVE:

REFLECTIONS ON CHRIST'S SUFFERINGS AND DEATH

DR. DAVID EWERT

TABLE OF CONTENTS

Preface 3

1. Preparing for the Passion (Mark 14:1-9) 5

2. The Last Supper (Mark 14:10-21) 17

3. The Lord's Supper (Mark 14:22-31) 27

4. Gethsemane (Mark 14:3242) 38

5. The Betrayal and Arrest of Jesus (Mark 14:43-52) 53

6. Jesus' Trial By the Sanhedrin (Mark 14:53-65) 64

7. Peter's Denial of His Lord (Mark 14:66-72) 76

8. Jesus Before the Governor (Mark 15:1-15) 86

9. They Crucified Him (Mark 15:16-26) 99

10. Christ's Death on the Cross (Mark 15:2741) 111

11. The Burial and Resurrection of Jesus (Mark 15:42-16:8) 124

Preface

The high point of the Christian year is Passion week. The suffering and death of Christ is the focal point in salvation history, and the Passion narratives of our Gospel writers comprise the very heart of the gospel. The gospel is called "the word of the cross" (1 Cor 1:18). In his brief summary of the gospel in his first letter to the Corinthians, the apostle Paul writes, "For I handed on to you as of first importance what I in turn had received: that Christ died for our sins in accordance with the scriptures, and that he was buried, and that he was raised on the third day in accordance with the scriptures (15:3,4).

For a religion to mark its beginning with the crucifixion of its founder is exceedingly strange. But for the past two millennia the story of Christ's suffering and death has fascinated people all over the world. From every angle that people might look at the Passion story, it grabs them. In his massive work on The Death of the Messiah (p. viii), Raymond Brown illustrates the centrality and significance of the Passion narrative: Seen from the aesthetic side, there is nothing in the Gospels that has given us such glorious music, or has inspired such magnificent art, as the Passion story. From the literary point of view, this story has even entered our everyday language. People still speak of a "Judas kiss," of selling Christ for 30 pieces of silver, of washing our hands of an embarrassing situation — all found in the Passion story.

From the historical standpoint, no event in Christ's public life was seen by so many eye witnesses. From the first century up to the present, churches around the world have recited the Apostles Creed, in which they affirm that Christ "suffered under Pontius Pilate." The death of Christ is an unassailable historical event on which the Christian faith rests.

Seen from a theological point of view, the Passion story assures us that through the death of Christ our sins have been atoned for, and that we have been delivered from death and despair through the death of an innocent substitute. That Jesus of Nazareth was crucified under Pontius Pilate can be discovered also from the Roman historian, Tacitus, but that he died for our sins is something only the gospel can tell us. Moreover, the Passion story has always been at the centre of Christian devotion and meditation, and the church loses much, if it overlooks the wonderful opportunity to proclaim the message of the cross, especially at Eastertide.

Preaching from narrative material, however, is not always easy, and the following chapters were written, in part, to illustrate how this moving story of Christ's suffering and death can be presented in sermon form. However, these meditations were written also with the Christian reader in mind, who may not have access to some of the rich literature that is available in this area of NT studies.

There is some disagreement among scholars over where precisely the Passion narrative begins. Not all would include, as I have, the anointing of Jesus at Bethany and the Last Supper. However, even though the actual sufferings of Christ began in Gethsemane, these accounts are an integral part of the Passion story. We will follow basically the Marcan account of Christ's suffering but weave in some materials from other Gospels to round out the picture.

It is our hope and prayer that these studies will serve as a handbook for teachers and preachers as they expound the Passion narrative. However, these reflections on the accounts of Christ's suffering, death and resurrection, may also be of help to serious Bible readers who are interested in a devotional approach to the biblical text. Although I have refrained from injecting bibliographical information into these studies, I am indebted to many scholars who have painstakingly examined Mark's account of our Lord's Passion.

David Ewert, Professor Emeritus of Biblical Studies, Canadian Mennonite University; Winnipeg, Manitoba.

Chapter 1

Preparing for the Passion Mark 14: 1-9

The anointing of Jesus at Bethany marks the beginning of the Passion narrative in the Synoptic Gospels. However, the shadow of the cross hung over the life and ministry of Jesus almost from the very beginning of the Gospel story. In Mark 3:6 we read, that "the Pharisees went out and immediately conspired with the Herodians against him, how to destroy Jesus." It is then not altogether surprising, when some biblical scholars have suggested that our Gospels are really Passion narratives with long introductions.

There is no doubt that the Passion story is the very heart of the Gospel. If our Gospels were simply biographies of Jesus, we would have expected the writers to devote more space to the life of Jesus. But they skip over the first 30 years of his life, describe his three-year ministry, and then give an elaborate account of his suffering and death. Some time ago I read an 800-page biography of the famous German NT scholar, Adolf Schlatter, whose books were widely used by Mennonite ministers of a former generation. Only two pages at the end of this huge volume are devoted to a report on the death of Schlatter.

The story of Christ's death would, of course, have never been written up, had he not risen from the dead. If Christ had remained in the grave, the whole movement which he had begun would have ended in failure and disappointment. But because he arose triumphantly from the dead, the authors of our Gospels write the tragic story of Christ's suffering and death without embarrassment. The Easter sun streams through the accounts of Christ's passion.

It is widely held by scholars that the Passion narrative was the first part of the Gospel story to be put into writing. We should remember that our Gospels were written a whole generation after our Lord went to glory. The Gospel stories circulated in oral form during this early period. Then, beginning in the sixties, the Gospels were put to writing.

The Passion narrative in the Gospels is a poweful piece of writing. Many an unbeliever has been brought to Christ simply by reading or hearing the Passion story. Dr. Norman Snaith, a famous British OT scholar, and author of a number of books, was an atheist in his college days. He had severed all ties to religion and the church. Then one day he turned to the NT. Being conversant with the biblical languages, he read the Passion story in the original Greek, and God invaded his life and he became a humble follower of Christ. Other examples of people who committed their lives to Christ after reading the Passion story, could be given.

In the following pages we want to trace the footsteps of Jesus, as he walks into the jaws of death. Luke writes, "when his time had come, he set his face to go to Jerusalem" (9:51).

On the way to Jerusalem he had repeatedly explained to his disciples, that he would be betrayed and killed, and they found that hard to believe. Peter, in fact, protested strongly when our Lord made this ominous prediction. They had come to believe that Jesus was the Messiah, and they could not yet integrate Messiah's death into their theology. But now the hour had struck—the hour for which our Lord had come into this world.

Before he began to walk through the valley of the shadow of death, he spent a delightful time among friends. On this occasion Mary, whose home he had visited on former occasions, demonstrates her love for Christ, by pouring a container of costly perfume on our Lord's head. And Jesus interprets her extravagant act of kindness as a preparation for his burial. And so we want to look upon this account as a preparation for Christ's passion.

I. THE HISTORICAL CONTEXT

A. The Plot to Kill Jesus (vv. 1,2). "It was two days before the Passover and the festival of Unleavened Bread. The chief priests and the scribes were looking for a way to arrest him by stealth and kill him; for they said, 'Not during the festival, or there may be a riot among the people'."

How long Jesus had already been in Jerusalem is not known, but just before Passover, which was always celebrated on Thursday evening, the Jewish hierarchy plotted his death. The feast of Unleavened Bread began with Passover and ran for a week, and so Passover and Unleavened Bread are often drawn together as one festival.

Jerusalem was crowded with Jewish visitors from all over the Roman world. It is estimated that the population of Jerusalem quadrupled at this time of the year, around the end of March. Jerusalem was declared common property of all Jewry for this festival week, and so lodging was not a serious problem for visitors. At Passover, messianic hopes and nationalistic feelings always ran high, as the Jews relived their deliverance from slavery in Egypt long ago.

Prudence would have counselled Jesus to stay away from Jerusalem at Passover, or at least to remain hidden in the back streets. But that is precisely what he would not do. God's hour had struck and his public and triumphal entry into the city, recorded in Mark 11, makes that clear.

The Jewish Sanhedrin was bent on killing this radical Galilean, whose teaching turned their religious practices and traditions upside down. But they also realized that Jesus was extremely popular with the common folk, and decided not to arrest him secretly and kill him during the festival, in order not to provoke a riot among the populace. Evidently they had decided to wait until after the festival, but something unexpected happened that changed their plans. Judas, one of the Twelve, offered to betray Jesus. It was an offer they could not refuse.

As the storm clouds gathered around our Lord's head, he visited his friends in Bethany. It must have warmed his heart to be invited for dinner by people who held him in deep respect and esteem.

B. The Home in Bethany (v.3). "While he was at Bethany in the house of Simon the leper, as he sat at table, a woman came with an alabaster jar of very costly ointment of nard, and she broke open the jar and poured the ointment on his head."

In John's Gospel we are told that it was Mary who anointed Jesus, and that Martha served at the dinner, and that Lazarus was one of those who sat at table with Jesus. Here we are told that the dinner was given in the house of Simon, the leper. There are a dozen men mentioned in the NT who bear the common Jewish name, Simon. Nicknames were often used to distinguish one from another. This Simon is known as "the leper." Whether he was still alive or not is not known, but the dinner was in his house. It has been suggested that he was one of the lepers whom Jesus had healed, but that he was still known by this nickname, somewhat like Matthew who continued to be known as tax-collector. The word "leprosy" covers all kinds of diseases and so we do not know precisely what Simon's situation was or had been.

How kind of these friends to open their hearts and their home to the Master, just before the cruel hate of his enemies would attempt to put out the light of life! Jesus was reclining at table, when Mary poured the ointment over his head. In Jesus' day people normally sat when they partook of food. Standing was forbidden by Jewish custom. That was the posture of the slave. Once in Egypt, on the first Passover night, they had stood, ready for the exodus. But never again. At formal meals, however, the reclining position was common. People lay on divans, leaning on the left arm and eating with the right. On this occasion, as Jesus and the other guests reclined, Mary came from behind, carrying a container of concentrated perfume in an alabaster flask. These flasks, made of glassy marble, had long necks. By sealing the flask the fragrance was maintained. Mark reports that she broke the flask, which no doubt means the neck of the flask, and poured the contents on Jesus. I would like to call this the extravagance of Mary.

II. THE EXTRAVAGANCE OF MARY

"She broke open the jar and poured the ointment on his head"(v. 3b). We are told that important people were sometimes honored by breaking the cup from which they had drunk, so that no one else would ever drink from it. The colt on which Jesus rode was one on which no one else had ridden. The tomb in which Jesus was laid was one in which no one else had ever lain.

It was not unusual for guests at a festive occasion to have their heads anointed by the host. When Jesus accepted an invitation for dinner from Simon the Pharisee, and a woman off the street anointed Jesus' feet, Simon was upset. Jesus then reminded him that he had neglected to anoint Jesus' head with oil (Lk 7). That was part of common etiquette and courtesy. But here we have something unusual.

Not only did she pour the ointment of nard on Jesus' head but, according to John's Gospel, she also anointed his feet and then wiped them with her hair, rather than with a towel. This is all the more striking, for Jewish women did not unbind their hair in public; in fact they normally covered it with a kerchief or shawl. This was an extravagant demonstration of love and loyalty to Jesus.

Bible readers have often wondered what may have

motivated her. She had had encounters with Jesus before. In John 11 we have the account of the death of her brother Lazarus and his resurrection from the dead. He was present now, sitting at table (Jo 12:2). Could it be that they were celebrating his return to life? This may have been Mary's way of saying thanks. In Luke 10 we have that memorable occasion when Jesus visited Lazarus and his sisters in their home, and Mary sat at his feet and listened to his teachings. That may be a Hebraic way of saying that she was a disciple: to sit at the master's feet. And, in contrast to the disciples of Jesus, she seems to have accepted the fact that Jesus was to suffer and die.

Given the costliness of the unguent which she poured out on Jesus, she must have saved and scrounged for a long time, waiting for the right moment to honor the Master before he died. This opportunity had now come, and so she poured a pound of costly perfume on Jesus. Her act was so artless and unsophisticated. Without calculating the cost, she demonstrated her love for the Savior. And the house was full of the fragrance — a fragrance that two millennia of time have not yet erased.

From Mary's generosity we turn now to the negative reaction of some of the disciples. According to John's Gospel it was Judas who spoke for the rest of the disciples. Mark limits the criticism to some of the guests, but Matthew says simply "the disciples" We must assume, then, that Judas was speaking on behalf of all of them.

III. THE REACTION OF THE DISCIPLES

"But some were there who said to one another in anger, 'Why was the ointment wasted in this way? For this ointment could have been sold for more than three hundred denarii and the money given to the poor.' And they scolded her" (vv. 4,5).

Judas and the other disciples saw Mary's act of devotion as a thoughtless waste; it was sheer recklessness. According to Matthew 20:2 a laborer in those days was paid one denarius a day. Mary had squandered 300 denarii — roughly a year's wages. She had taken leave of her senses and thrown caution to the wind. When Jesus asked his disciples to provide bread for 5000, Philip suggested that 200 denarii would probably not be enough to feed them. Perhaps that helps us to put the value of 300 denarii in perspective.

Normally Peter is the spokesman for the Twelve, but this time it's Judas, as John's Gospel clearly states. And that Evangelist then adds this devastating comment: "He said this not because he cared about the poor, but because he was a thief; he kept the common purse and used to steal what was put into it" (Jo 12:6). This love of money led him eventually to betray Jesus for 30 pieces of silver. His mind had been warped by greed. And the Italian poet, Dante, in The Divine Comedy puts Judas in the lowest hell, the hell of ice and snow, reserved for cool, calculating, deliberate sinners. Judas did not appreciate Mary's loving, sacrificial act. And his fellow-disciples agreed with him. Mark says, "they scolded her."

When Albert Schweitzer decided to go to Africa, Christian friends (including ministers) cautioned him against throwing his great gifts and learning away. Trained in music, philosophy and theology, he took up the study of medicine somewhat later in life, because he saw in Africa the modern Lazarus whom God had put on Europe's doorstep. But had he not thrown his life away, as some thought of it, we probably wouldn't know all that much about him today.

Our story, fortunately, does not end with the sharp criticism of the disciples, but with the defense of Mary's extravagant act by Jesus. Let us look at Jesus' response!

IV. THE RESPONSE OF JESUS

A. He Gives Mary's Deed a Profound Meaning (vv. 6 and 8). "But Jesus said, 'Let her alone; why do you trouble her? She has performed a good service for me... She has done what she could; she has anointed my body beforehand for its burial'."

Jesus rises to her defense. First he tells the disciples to leave her alone and not to cause her further pain. And then he stresses the significance of such good deeds. The word "good" (***kalos***) can also be translated as lovely, beautiful, winsome, noble. What she had done was not only morally good, but it was also a goodness pleasant to behold—a goodness that strikes the eye.

Jesus and the apostles make it explicitly clear in their teachings, that no one will enter the gates of heaven because of the good deeds they have done. However, they are also united in pointing out, that good deeds are the sign of a genuine faith. John, in the Revelation, explains that those who die in the Lord rest from their labors, but "their deeds follow them" (Rev 14:13). Faith and works are intimately linked with each other. In the same book, John describes the wedding dress of the bride of Christ, which she wears at the marriage supper of the Lamb (Rev 19:8); it is "her righteous deeds."

Not only does Jesus recognize the nobility of Mary's act, but he also gives it a profound significance with respect to his own life. He says that she did this "for him" (v. 6). Moreover, he says, "she did what she could"(v. 8). And that is a very encouraging remark for all of us who often feel that we can't do what others can. She did what she could. God does not expect of us what we cannot give.

But Jesus said even more. "She has anointed my body beforehand for its burial." Did Mary know that? Did she expect Jesus to be put to death like those whose body would not be anointed? She seems to have understood better than the Twelve, that Jesus was about to face death. Later, after Christ's body had been laid into a tomb, other women came to anoint his body, but they came too late; he had risen from the dead. Mary had done this noble deed in advance.

In any case, Jesus gives a deep meaning to a very humble act, that of pouring precious nard on his head and on his feet. And so it will always be in the kingdom of God: simple acts of love, inspired by devotion to the Savior, have profound significance. Jesus said that even a cup of cold water, given in his name would not go unrewarded.

But Jesus had even more so say: he also made an important observation on the necessity of caring for the needy.

B. He Endorses the Concern for the Needy (v.7).

"For you always have the needy with you, and you can show kindness to them whenever you wish; but you will not always have me."

Judas and his fellow disciples thought Mary had been wasteful; the money could have been used to help the poor. It was a custom that at Passover, people were to offer the poor some help. In John 13:29 we read that when Judas left the table in the upper room, where Jesus was celebrating the last supper with his disciples, some of them thought he was leaving to give something to the poor, since he carried the purse. But the apostle John also says, that Judas wasn't really concerned about the poor, but rather about the loss of three hundred denarii. Jesus picks up on that hypocritical remark and puts it into right perspective.

The language Jesus uses ("the poor are always with you") comes from Deuteronomy 15:11. Because there would always be poor people, Israel was exhorted to have an open heart for the needy. This saying should, however, not be interpreted to mean, that it is God's will that there should always be poor people. That there are poor people and rich people is not a divinely instituted order of society. In the 19th century the Chartists in England worked for the betterment of the poor, but didn't find much support from the churches. The inequities between social classes in England were often explained as a God-ordained arrangement. Some church leaders condemned the Chartists because poverty, they said, was "the result of the everlasting purpose of a Sovereign God," and not because of unjust human laws. This misconception was immortalized by Mrs. Alexander, who wrote of "The rich man in his castle, the poor man at his gate. God made them high and lowly, and ordered their estate."

But that's not the way the early church read these words of Jesus. From the time the apostolic church was established at Pentecost, the believers were concerned about the needy. And the apostle Paul never forgot the poor in his efforts to bring the gospel to the ends of the earth.

In the Decian persecutions, in the middle of the 3rd century, the police broke into a church in Rome, hoping to find money. And when they asked the deacons where the church's treasures were hidden, they pointed to the hundreds of widows and orphans that were being fed daily by the church. "There," they said, "are our treasures."

Some years ago the Christian senator, Mark Hatfield of Oregon, made a public plea, asking Americans to reduce waste and to live more frugally, so that more could be done for the poor of this world. A reader of the Moody Monthly responded with a letter in which he argued: "Our first charge from the Lord Jesus is to preach the gospel. There's no command to feed the world. You know (Mr. Hatfield) according to God's word, the poor are with us always...." But that's not the teaching of either the Old Testament or the New. The tension between evangelism and concern for the poor is not to be found in the teachings and ministry of the apostles.

Jesus' comment on Mary's noble deed becomes the occasion for the prediction of Jesus, that his followers would some day be engaged in bringing the gospel to the ends of the earth.

C. He Foresees the World Mission of the Church (v. 9). "Truly I tell you that wherever the good news is proclaimed in the whole world, what she has done will be told in remembrance of her."

Mary anointed Jesus for his burial. But death would not have the last word to say. Jesus looks beyond the grave and the resurrection to the day when his followers would carry the gospel into the whole world. Until now Jesus had limited his mission quite deliberately to the lost sheep of the house of Israel. But once the work of redemption would be completed, and the Spirit would be poured out, Christ's faithful witnesses would begin in Jerusalem and bring the gospel to the ends of the earth (Acts 1:8). The world mission lay beyond the cross.

And it didn't take long before the good news reached the Samaritans (Acts 8), and the Gentiles (Acts 10) in Palestine. But then it crossed the borders and spread to all the provinces of the sprawling Roman empire. By the end of the first century the Christian faith had spread throughout the known world. And since then it has penetrated almost every corner of the globe. And wherever the gospel has been proclaimed, Jesus' prediction has been fulfilled: the story of Mary's loving deed, embedded in three of our Gospels, was told.

It is sometimes said that the apostles expected an almost immediate end to the present age and the return of Christ in glory. And it is true, they labored with the understanding that time was short. But they also knew that Jesus had predicted that there would be an interim between Pentecost and his Parousia at the end of the age. During this interim the church would carry out its mission. Jesus said in his Olivet Discourse, "This gospel of the kingdom will be proclaimed throughout the world, as a testimony to all the nations; and then the end will come" (Mt 24:14).

This mission has not yet been completed. But wherever Christ's messengers go to proclaim the good news of salvation, they also tell the story of Mary's act of devotion to Jesus. Christians all over the world know this story. They may not know much about Alexander the Great, about Herod the Great, or about Julius Caesar, or some other famous character of the ancient world. But they know about Mary; who shone like a brilliant light in that dark hour of Jesus' life, when he was surrounded by treachery and hatred.

And so, as we remember Christ's passion during this Easter season, let us be encouraged by Mary's costly act of devotion. But let us also be warned by the reaction of Judas, lest our vision be distorted by greed and avarice. And let us be encouraged by the wonderful words of Jesus, who gives meaning to even insignificant acts of love. Above all, let us not fail in our concern for the needy, and our calling to bring the gospel to those who have not yet heard.

Chapter 2

The Last Supper Mark 10:10-21

Some years ago the New Testament scholar I. Howard Marshall of Aberdeen published a book with the title, Last Supper and Lord's Supper. In this book he asks his readers to distinguish clearly between the "last supper" which Jesus ate with his disciples before his death, and the "Lord's Supper" which was instituted on that occasion. The "last supper" was a Jewish Passover meal at which Israel's redemption from Egyptian bondage was remembered, reenacted. It was at such a meal that Jesus inaugurated the new covenant, and when the new people of God, the church, celebrates Communion, the Lord's Supper, it commemorates its deliverance from the bondage of sin.

In Mark 14:22ff, we have an account of the institution of the Lord's Supper and we will focus on that in our next sermon. Today, however, we want to concentrate on the last supper that Jesus ate before he entered Gethsemane, before he was captured, tried and crucified. After repeatedly telling his disciples that he was going up to Jerusalem where he would be rejected by the Jewish rulers, would suffer and be killed, that hour had now arrived.

Last meals with friends and loved ones are usually clouded somewhat with a spirit of heaviness, but in the case of the last supper that Jesus ate with his disciples, the mood was extremely sombre. First, because Jesus was about to suffer and die, and second, because this Passover celebration was saddened by the shameful betrayal of Jesus by one of his disciples. Our passage begins and ends with a brief account of this betrayal.

I. THE TREACHERY OF JUDAS

"Then Judas Iscariot, who was one of the twelve, went to the chief priests in order to betray him" (v. 10). If this account were not authentic, our Gospel writers would not have included it. It must have been embarrassing and painful for the Evangelists, who gave us our Gospels, to report the betrayal of Jesus by one of the Twelve. Mark omits any reference to a possible motive on the part of Judas for this despicable deed; other Gospels attribute it to greed or even to Satanic inspiration.

In order to distinguish the Judas who betrayed Jesus, from the other Judas who belonged to the Twelve (who was the son of James, Acts 1:13), he is identified as "Iscariot." The word "Iscariot" could possibly mean "the man (*ish* in Hebrew) from Kerioth," but there are other possibilities. Mark adds, "who was one of the Twelve." That reminds us of that memorable event mentioned at the beginning of his Gospel, when Jesus appointed the Twelve (Mk 3:16-19), among whom was Judas "who betrayed him." On that occasion, when Jesus chose his disciples, they "came to him" (Mk 3:13), and Judas also left the crowd and entered into fellowship with Jesus. But now Judas "goes away" to the chief priests; he leaves the fellowship of Jesus. To be sure he will come to the table with Jesus and the other disciples at the last supper, but as an outsider, as a betrayer.

In the account of the anointing of Jesus, Mary sacrifices a year's earnings to express her devotion to Jesus; Judas accepts money to betray him. Festival pilgrims handed over their lambs to the priests, who would slaughter them; Judas hands over Jesus, the Lamb of God, to be killed at the instigation of the Jewish high priests.

Judas goes to the chief priests, which in this case means the Sanhedrin, with the deliberate purpose of betraying him to them. Mark began his Passion narrative (14:1,2) with a reference to the plot of the Jewish leaders to arrest Jesus by stealth and to kill him. However, they had to take into account Jesus' popularity among the common people and so they decided not to carry out their wicked plan during the Passover festival. Jerusalem's population quadrupled during Passover and the presence of excitable Galileans added to the volatility of the crowds. According to an OT law (Deut 17:23) a heretic was to he killed "before the people," as a warning to others, but in the case of Jesus that would possibly spark a riot. Evidently, then, they had decided to carry out their sinister plot after the festival. But then something happened that changed their mind: Judas came to them and offered to betray Jesus. Now they saw a way of getting rid of Jesus without causing an uproar.

"When they heard it, they were greatly pleased, and promised to give him money. So he began to look for an opportunity to betray him" (v.11). Evidently Judas thought he could turn Jesus over to them in relative secrecy, so that there would be no great disturbance at the festival. Of course, he would carry out his plot only for a price. And when he asked the chief priests how much they were willing to give him (Mt 27:15), they offered him thirty pieces of silver. Assuming that each piece of silver was the equivalent of a denarius (although that is not certain), then this was one-tenth of the amount that Mary had spent in order to lavish her love on the Master and in that way anoint him for his burial (v.8). Mark shows remarkable restraint in the details of this tragic event. Matthew and Luke add that he made a solid bargain.

Having promised Judas this paltry sum, he now decides to return to Jesus and his band of disciples, to find out secretly what Jesus planned to do, and where he would be in the next day or so. Passover had to be eaten within the confines of Jerusalem and, whereas Jesus had spent the previous nights in

Bethany, he would remain in the city on Passover night. It remained only to discover where Jesus planned to eat the Passover meal and where he would spend the rest of the night. Once he knew that, the rest of his plot would fall into place. At the last supper he found out where Jesus and his disciples were going to spend the night (Jo 18:1,2), and he then made arrangements for Jesus' capture. From this account of the treachery of Judas, Mark now takes us to the place where Jesus will eat the last supper with his own.

II. THE PREPARATION FOR THE MEAL

A. The Time of the Preparation (v. 12). "On the first day of Unleavened Bread, when the Passover lamb is sacrificed, his disciples said to him' 'Where do you want us to go and make the preparations for you to eat the Passover'?"

Passover and the festival of Unleavened Bread belonged together. On a Thursday morning the houses of Jews would be cleaned of all leaven and so by evening, when the Passover meal was eaten, they ate it with unleavened bread. Although Passover was celebrated on the 14th of Nisan, by evening it was already the 15th, for the Jews counted days from evenings rather than from mornings. In the week following, only unleavened bread was eaten. On Thursday afternoon the Passover lambs were brought to the temple. Here their throats were slit and the blood was dashed against the altar. After they were skinned and the entrails and the fat were extracted, the carcasses were handed back to the owners, who took them home to be roasted.

During Passover, Jerusalem was declared to be common property of all Jewry and so hospitality was offered readily to the many visitors that crowded into the city at this time. Jesus, for some reason, had waited right to the last to make arrangements for the last supper, and so the disciples ask him where he intended to celebrate Passover. Whether Jesus or one of his friends had the lamb slaughtered in the temple, or whether he intended to eat the last supper without lamb, is not certain. Because there was a price on his head, it would have been too risky to go to the temple with the sacrificial lamb. Jesus then gives rather detailed instructions regarding arrangements for the supper.

B. The Place to Be Prepared (vv. 13-16). To begin with (v. 12) the disciples took the initiative and asked Jesus where he wanted them to prepare the meal, but now it appears as if he had made advance arrangements himself. The story is not designed to portray Jesus' foreknowledge (although he had such knowledge). Rather, the prior arrangements had been made so that the venue would remain a secret until Jesus had finished the Passover meal with his disciples.

He now gives two of his disciples (Peter and John, according to Luke) a commission, saying, "Go into the city, and a man carrying a water jar will meet you; follow him." Residents of Jerusalem would draw their water from the pool of Siloam and perhaps the disciples were instructed to go there. For a man to carry an earthen jug with water would be a most unusual sight, for carrying water from a well was considered to be a woman's duty. Men might carry leather bottles with water or wineskins, but not pots on their head. Perhaps a modern parallel might be if a man were seen carrying a large women's purse or a colorful women's umbrella.

The two messengers were to follow this man to his house and then say to him, "The Teacher asks, Where is my guest room where I may eat the Passover with my disciples?" (v.14). When Jesus spoke of "his" guest room he did not mean that he was the owner of this particular house, but that he had agreed in advance with the owner to make use of this facility. Jerusalem residents were forbidden to charge for the use of their facilities by visitors at Passover season. (Guests often rewarded the owner of the house by giving him the hide of the sacrificial   lamb.)

The owner of this house must have been a very courageous man, for he had agreed to shelter the "heretical" Galilean and his outlawed company of followers. It has been suggested that perhaps it was the householder who had gone to the temple to have the Passover lamb slaughtered, and who had provided the other requirements for the meal.

Assuming that Jesus planned to eat a regular Passover with his disciples, they would need saltwater, matzos, bitter herbs, haroset, wine, greens such as parsley or celery. Mark leaves such details to the side, for he is not out to describe in detail a Jewish Passover. Rather, he wants to describe the last supper at which the Lord's Supper was instituted.

Jesus had predicted also that the owner of the house would show them an "upper room," where Jesus would be able to celebrate Passover undisturbed. Larger Jewish houses had upper rooms. They were somewhat like a smaller box on top of a bigger one and were approached by an outside stairway. They served a variety of purposes. Rabbis sometimes taught their students in such upper rooms. When it is said that this large upper room was furnished, we must assume that table and divans, as well as the necessary dishes were available. By now, of course the house was free from all leaven.

"So the disciples set out and went to the city, and found everything as he had told them; and they prepared the Passover meal" (v.16). Whether the disciples got any help from women folk in the preparation of the meal is not stated, nor is it known whether any were present at the last supper. It was thought generally that one roasted lamb was sufficient for about ten participants. With the arrangements made, we are now ready to follow Jesus and his disciples to the upper room where they will eat the Passover. In the course of eating the meal, Jesus speaks some ominous words about his betrayal by one of his disciples.

III. THE PROPHECY OF THE BETRAYAL

A. The Prediction (vv. 17,18). "When it was evening, he came with the twelve. And when they had taken their places and were eating, Jesus said, 'Truly I tell you, one of you will betray me'."

Passover, in contrast to ordinary suppers, began at 6 p.m., according to our time, and was to be over by midnight. It had to be eaten within the walls of Jerusalem, and so Jesus and his disciples came from Bethany to the city to eat the Passover. Whether the two disciples had returned to Bethany is not known, but they are part of the apostolic band, as was Judas. Mark simply says, that when it was evening he came "with the twelve." Three times Mark mentions "the twelve" in our passage. It seems to heighten the enormity of what was happening — that one of the twelve should betray him.

As Jesus and his disciples entered the upper room, they took their places. Literally the verb (Gr. *anakeimai*) means to recline. It was custom that guests at formal meals lay on divans on their left side and partook of the food with their right hand. The food would be served on low tables. Normally people sat at meals, but Passover was different. Reclining was a sign of a free person. On the night of the exodus from Egypt they had stood as they ate unleavened bread, because of the urgency of the hour. To stand while eating was thought to be a sign of slavery. But now the Jews were free (even though they were under Roman rule).

It was custom, after the guests had reclined, for the pater familias to take a cup of wine and to speak a blessing. The first cup was then passed around. Altogether four cups were to be emptied, to remind the participants of the four promises of deliverance which God had given Israel at the time of the exodus from Egypt (Ex 6:6,7). After the first cup, food was brought in, consisting of unleavened bread, bitter herbs, greens, stewed fruit and roast lamb. There followed then a rehearsal of the exodus event through question and answer, followed by the recitation of Psalms 113-114, the first part of the so-called Hallel (praise). This was followed by the second cup. The head of the household would then take the bread, break it and hand pieces to the participants who ate it with the bitter herbs and stewed fruit. The main meal, of course, included also roasted lamb. After the main meal a third cup was passed around, called "the cup of blessing." There were also prayers and blessings spoken throughout. Finally the second part of the Hallel (Pss 116- 118) was recited, followed by the fourth cup which concluded the Passover ceremony.

At the last supper, the festivity of the meal was shattered when Jesus predicted that one of his disciples, who was present at the table and eating with him, would betray him (v. 18). These must have been among the most difficult words Jesus ever spoke. When he called the twelve to apostleship, Mark tells us in 3:14, that they should be "with him." Notice the repetition of this phrase in our text. Jesus comes "with the twelve" (v. 17); "the one eating with me" (v. 18); "the one who dips into the bowl with me" (v. 20). To eat together was a symbol of fellowship, of family, of covenant. And in this intimate circle of Jesus' followers is one who will betray his Master. The word "betray" can also be translated as "to give over," and it probably has a double nuance in our text. Judas will betray his Lord, and Christ will be given over by God into the hands of sinners.

B. The Consternation (vv. 19,20). The prediction of Jesus, that one of the twelve would betray him, was so shocking to his disciples, that they began to grieve deeply. "They began to be distressed and so say to him one after another, 'Surely not I'?" (v. 19). It was a word of protest; the very suggestion that anyone would betray Jesus hurt and puzzled them. Perhaps there was also an element of doubt in their question, for the question assumes a negative answer. Jesus then went on to identify the betrayer.

"He said to them, 'It is one of the twelve, one who is dipping bread into the bowl with me" (v.20). The word "bread" is not mentioned in the Greek text, but perhaps it is implied. Pieces of unleavened bread were dipped into the bowl containing the haroset. (This was made of apples, nuts, cinnamon and wine. Its color was reminiscent of the clay the slaves used to make bricks for Pharaoh's pyramids.) That Jesus would dip bread into the bowl together with Judas, shows the depth of his love. It is even possible that it was Jesus' last appeal to Judas, not to carry out his nefarious designs. But Judas, so it seems, was already past hope. John reports that when Jesus gave Judas a piece of the bread, Satan entered into him (Jo 13:27).

It is sometimes argued by people who have been brought up in a strict Calvinist tradition, in which the eternal security of the believer is confessed, that Judas had never been a follower of Christ. But that's not the impression we get from the Gospels. Moreover, the NT does speak of the awful possibility of falling away from Christ. And so the apostasy of Judas must for all times remain as a warning sign for all true believers.

C. The Observation (v. 21). Our passage ends with a profound observation made by Jesus. First, he puts his death into the context of God's saving plans: "for the Son of Man goes as it is written of him." The "going away" of which Jesus spoke was a reference to his death. He was on his way to Calvary. And by his death scripture would be fulfilled. He doesn't refer to any scripture passage in particular, but the OT had much to say about the suffering servant of Yahweh (cf. Isa 53). It looks as if Jesus combined Daniel 7:13,14, where the heavenly Son of Man is mentioned, with Isaiah 53, where the servant of Yahweh lays down his life for others. Jesus, as it were, transfers what was said of the suffering servant to the Son of Man mentioned in Daniel.

However, even though Christ's death was in God's eternal plan, there was no excuse for Judas's treachery. "But woe to that man by whom the Son of Man is betrayed! It would have been better for that one not to have been born." The "woe" expressed by Jesus is not a curse, but a cry of pain and commiseration. The betrayer is morally responsible for his evil deed, even though Christ's death was in God's plan. And even when it is said that Satan entered Judas, that does not let Judas off the hook. With great sadness Jesus makes the observation, that it would have been better for Judas, had he never been born.

We have here a paradox of Scripture: "The Son of Man is betrayed by a friend in fulfillment of Scripture, and yet this friend is culpable for his act. Judas cannot escape personal responsibility for his action. The apostle Peter in his Pentecostal message (Acts 2:23) shows his grasp of this paradox, when he condemns the action of his countrymen in betraying Christ to the Gentiles, who then killed him, and yet sees all of this also as taking place in the plan and foreknowledge of God.

Judas is a tragic figure. He began his life in fellowship with Jesus with high promise but, because he opened his heart to Satan's wiles, his life ended in tragedy. What can we say but, "there for the grace of God go I."

Chapter 3

The Lord's Supper Mark 14:22-31

    The earliest account of the institution of the Lord's Supper is found in 1 Corinthians 11:23-25. This letter, which Paul wrote to the Corinthians about two decades after Christ's death, was published earlier than our Gospels. However, all the accounts of the last supper, at which Christ instituted what came to be called "the Lord's Supper," go back to that historical event in Jerusalem when our Lord, together with his disciples, partook of a Jewish Passover meal. To be sure Paul writes that he received it "from the Lord," but that is not a reference to a special divine revelation given to Paul, but rather, that he had received the tradition of the institution of the Lord's Supper which went back to Jesus.
    The difference between the Pauline account of the institution of the Lord's Supper and that of the Gospels is, that Paul focuses on the bread and the cup and their significance, and gives the church a few guidelines on the celebration of Communion. The Gospels, on the other hand, give us the historical setting in which the Lord's Supper was instituted. There are also minor differences between the accounts in the Synoptic Gospels, but we will focus on the Marcan account today.
    Mark connects Jesus' prediction of the coming failure of the twelve and Peter's denial of his Lord, with the Last Supper. Whether Jesus made these predictions while they were still at the Passover table, or whether he made them on the way to

Gethsemane, is not quite certain. The account of the institution of the Lord's Supper ends with the comment, that they went out to the Mount of Olives. Be that as it may, we will include Jesus' prophecy of the breakdown of the loyalty of the twelve to their Master, under the topic of "The Lord's Supper." We want to follow the account as found in Mark and begin with the interpretation of the elements.

I. THE INTERPRETATION OF THE ELEMENTS (vv. 22-24)

It was a custom in Israel that the eating of the Passover meal included a rehearsal of the exodus event. This was a fixed part of the Passover liturgy. The head of the family would answer questions regarding the different items of food on the table. This was done before the meal was eaten. Very likely Jesus lifted a platter of unleavened bread and spoke a blessing over it. There would have been nothing unusual about that. But then something out of the ordinary occurred. Jesus gave the bread a new meaning, a new significance.

A. The Bread (v. 22). "While they were eating, he took the loaf of bread, and after blessing it he broke it, gave it to them, and said, 'Take; this is my body'."

In contrast to Matthew and Luke, who say that Jesus "thanked" (*eucharisteo*) for the bread, Mark says that he spoke a blessing *(eulogeo)*. There is, however, no fundamental difference between these two verbs. Moreover, Jesus would have prayed in Aramaic and the Semitic verb "to bless" (*barak*) may be rendered in Greek either as "bless" or "thank." A standard Jewish prayer of blessing reads as follows: "Praised by Thou, O Lord, Sovereign of the world, who causes bread to come forth from the earth." Those present would respond with "Amen." Mark doesn't say that he blessed the bread. Rather, he blessed God for the food.

After the blessing, the head of the family would break a

piece for each person present and it would be passed from hand to hand until it reached all those present. The distribution was normally done in complete silence. But on this occasion the silence was broken by the interpretation which Jesus gave. "Take," he said, "this is my body." Luke adds, "which is for you." Also, he has the command, " Do this in remembrance of me." Mark is unusually concise: "Take; this is my body."

There have been endless debates over the meaning of that saying of Jesus. Obviously when Jesus broke the bread and distributed it, it was still bread. There was nothing unusual about the breaking of the bread, for that was done regularly at mealtimes. And so we should not read into the verb "to break" the notion that Jesus had the breaking of his physical body in mind. Jesus did not transform himself into bread, nor did the bread transform itself into Jesus, as this is understood in Roman Catholic circles, where the doctrine of trans-substantiation is taught.

Jesus was speaking figuratively, symbolically. "This is my body" meant, "I am this bread" The word "body" is repeatedly used for the "self". For example, when Paul exhorts us to "present our bodies" to God (Rom 12:1), he means that we should give ourselves to God. And so, whenever the church celebrates the Lord's Supper and each member takes a piece of bread, God's people are assured of Christ's presence with them. Perhaps this can be illustrated in this way: Someone has a photograph of himself or herself, and shows it to a friend with the comment, "that's me."

That Christ had his imminent death in mind, when he said these words, is clear from the addition in Luke: "which is given for you." That is certainly the way Paul understood this saying. In 1 Corinthians 11:26 he writes: "For as often as you eat this bread and drink the cup, you proclaim the Lord's death until he comes." The bread no less than the cup spoke of Christ's death on behalf of lost humanity. Christ gave his body as a sacrifice for the sins of the world (cf. Heb 10:10).

B. The Cup (v. 23). "Then he took the cup, and after giving thanks he gave it to them, and all of them drank from it." Very likely it was the third of the four cups drunk at Passover. This cup was known as the "cup of blessing." Whereas Mark uses the verb "bless" in verse 22, he now switches to "thank." This clearly suggests that the two verbs were used interchangeably. The verb "thank" (*eucharisteo*) has given us the name Eucharist for the Lord's Supper. This cup was passed from one person to the next until all had drunk from it.

So far there was nothing out of the ordinary about passing out a cup of wine (usually mixed with water) at Passover. But on this occasion the silence is once more broken, and Jesus speaks words of interpretation, of meaning. "He said to them, 'This is my blood of the covenant, which is poured out for many'" (v. 24). Luke and Paul add that it was the "new" covenant that Christ was establishing.

Clearly the cup of wine which Jesus passed out to his disciples was not his blood, but it represented his blood. The pouring out of his blood, in this context, meant that he would give his life in sacrifice for others. By calling it the blood of the covenant we are reminded of the covenant which God made with Israel at Sinai (Ex 24:8), which was ratified by the sprinkling of blood. The word "covenant", however, reminds us also of the promise of Jeremiah, that God would some day establish a "new" covenant (Jer 31:31). Obviously Jesus was looking beyond his death at this point and foresaw the emergence of a new people of God. In fact, it has often been said, that the twelve who reclined with Jesus at the Passover table in the upper room on that memorable night, were the representatives of the new people of God.

When Mark quotes Jesus as saying that his blood was being poured out "for many," we should not read into that the doctrine of limited atonement. The word "many" in Hebrew/Aramaic is often used as the equivalent for "all." "Many" is an echo of Isaiah 53:12, where the suffering servant dies, bearing "the sins of many" (i.e., all). These words of Jesus remind us of that memorable saying of Jesus about the Son of Man, who came, as he put it, "not to be served but to serve, and to give his life a ransom for many" (Mk 10:45). Not all people accept Christ's offer of salvation, but his death atoned for the sins of every man, woman and child that is born.

Jesus and his disciples participated in a Jewish Passover meal. But this meal was transformed by Jesus on the night that he was betrayed. No doubt Jesus saw in this meal an occasion to have fellowship with his disciples, and he had looked forward to this event with great anticipation. Not only was it a fellowship meal, but, because it was the last meal of its kind that he would have with his disciples, it was also a farewell meal. At this meal Jesus distributed the bread and the wine as it was done at Jewish Passover meals, but he gave an interpretation to these elements that gave symbolic significance to the bread and the wine. The bread was interpreted as his body, i.e., himself, given to death for "the many," i.e., for the people as a whole. The blood was interpreted as inaugurating a new covenant, brought into being by the shedding of his own blood as a sacrificial offering for the sins of the world. What Mark doesn't record, is Jesus' command that this simple rite should be repeated by his followers. Luke, however reports that when Jesus distributed and interpreted the bread, he added: "Do this in remembrance of me" (Lk 22:19). Paul, in the earliest account of the institution of the Lord's Supper, adds, "until I come." The church is to celebrate the Lord's Supper until the day when it will be united with her Lord at the heavenly banquet.

After distributing the elements and giving them a deep significance, Jesus looks beyond the cross to his coming in glory.

II. THE SUPPER AND THE COMING KINGDOM

"Truly I tell you, I will never drink of the fruit of the vine until that day when I drink it new in the kingdom of God" (v. 15).

The word "truly" is a translation of the Semitic "Amen" (retained in the Greek text), and speaks of absolute confidence and authority. We may humbly add an Amen to our prayers and confessions, but Jesus begins many of his great messianic sayings with "Amen." (In John's Gospel we even have the double Amen!) There are 13 of these Amen sayings in Mark's Gospel and this is the twelfth. Jesus has no doubts about his triumph over death. There will be an interruption; he will no longer drink of the fruit of the vine, as he so often did with his disciples when he was on earth. But after this interim, however long it may be, he will drink it with his followers in the kingdom of God.

Since it was custom to drink the 4th cup of wine at the end of the Passover celebration, it has been suggested that Jesus did not drink this last cup. The background for drinking four cups at Passover was Exodus 6:6,7, where we have a four-fold promise given by God to Israel that he would rescue them from Egyptian bondage. If he did not drink the 4th cup, then perhaps he was suggesting that he would drink the 4th cup with them at the messianic banquet, the marriage supper of the Lamb, as it is called in Revelation 19:6-9. Perhaps he wanted to suggest that the meal which he and the disciples had just eaten was unfinished (the last cup was omitted), and that he would complete the communion with his followers in the consummation of the age, which Jesus called "that day" (Mk 14:25).

The promise that he would drink it new in the kingdom of God suggests that this is an eschatological promise. Not all scholars agree with that. There are those who think that Jesus was speaking of the period between the Last Supper and his resurrection, during which he would fast. We do know that Jesus ate and drunk after he arose from the dead (Acts 10:41). There were, of course, no more Passovers after Jesus' resurrection, at which he drank from the fruit of the wine. Forty days after his resurrection he ascended into glory.

On the whole it seems more correct to see in this saying of

Jesus a promise that, when God's kingdom comes in all its glory, he will, as it were, sit at table with his people and celebrate the triumph of the kingdom of God. The kingdom of God must be understood as God's reign over a people that acknowledge him as sovereign. This reign of God was inaugurated by the coming of Jesus, by his life, his teachings, his death and his exaltation. This kingdom, also called the kingdom of Christ, is a present reality today, for wherever people confess Christ as their Lord, they become members of his kingdom. However, this kingdom also has a future dimension. Paul says that God is calling us "into his own kingdom and his glory" (1 Thess 1:12), and it is the kingdom in all its fullness of glory that Jesus had in mind when he spoke of eating it new in God's kingdom.

Implied is that there will be an interim during which Jesus will be physically absent, but he will keep his own safe until that glorious day at the end of the age, when he will be present with them at the heavenly banquet table. The emphasis in Jesus' words does not lie on the length of his absence or on the difficulties his followers will face in the period between the cross and the end of this age, but rather it is a word of assurance that he will keep them in his hand and bring them to glory in the end. The many Lord's Suppers of the church here on earth, waiting for the Lord to return, are but preparatory celebrations of the great banquet in the kingdom that is to come. Jesus said he would drink it "new" on "that day." That day is none other than the one mentioned in Revelation 21:5, where God says, "Behold, I am making all things new."

The early Aramaic-speaking church has left us a prayer that was often spoken when believers celebrated the Lord's Supper, namely ***maranatha***. It means "Lord come" and probably had a double meaning. On the one hand, it was a prayer for Christ to be present at the table, somewhat in the sense of the table grace, "Come Lord Jesus be our guest." On the other hand, it was a prayer to come at the end of the age, a prayer for the parousia to take place. The last book of the Bible closes with this prayer of longing: "Surely I am coming soon"; "Amen, Come, Lord Jesus" (Rev 22:20).

Since the day that Christ conquered death and the glorified Christ poured out his Spirit at Pentecost, the new people of God that emerged, began to celebrate the Lord's Supper. And since those early days of the church, Christians of different races, cultures, and languages have gathered on the Lord's day, to partake of the bread and the wine in remembrance of what happened on that memorable Passover night. Some celebrate it with elaborate ceremonial, others with studied simplicity, some in stately cathedrals, others in humble cottages; sometimes in large congregations, and sometimes in small groups. Familiarity may have dulled our ears to the words of institution, but the disciples never forgot Jesus' words about the bread and the cup, and his promise that in the coming kingdom of God he would sit at table with those who love him.

III. THE CONCLUSION OF THE SUPPER.

"When they had sung the hymn, they went out to the Mount of Olives" (v. 26). It was custom among devout Jews to remain at the Passover table for some time after the meal was concluded, and to converse about God's acts of redemption in the past and about their hopes for future deliverance. This table-fellowship concluded with the singing of the second half of the Hallel Psalms (116-118). It was customary to sing the Hallel responsively, one member at the table would recite the text and the others would respond with Hallelujah. Psalm 118 includes the glorious promise, "I shall not die, but I shall live, and recount the deeds of the Lord" (v. 17). We can only imagine what went through Jesus' mind as he spoke or heard those words. There is even more in that Psalm that seemed so applicable to Jesus' situation as he faced death: "The stone that the builders rejected has become the chief cornerstone" (v. 22). With these prophetic words ringing in his ears, our Lord leaves the Passover table, confident that God will bring him through suffering and death to a triumphant resurrection from the dead and highly exalt him in the end.

One question that we cannot answer with certainty is, whether Jesus' prediction of Peter's denial of his Lord was made at the table, before they left for the Mount of Olives, or whether he spoke these solemn prophetic words on the way to Gethsemane. Verse 26 can be seen as the conclusion of Mark's report on the institution of the Lord's Supper, or the introduction to the prophecy of Peter's denial. Be that as it may, we will add these prophetic words, found in verses 27-31, to our text this morning.

IV. VICTORY BEYOND FAILURE AND DENIAL

A. The Failure of the Twelve (v. 27). "And Jesus said to them, You will all become deserters; for it is written, 'I will strike the shepherd and the sheep will be scattered'". The Greek verb *skandalizomai* (our word "scandal") can mean simply to stumble and fall. Here it means more; it probably means, that they will lose faith in Jesus and desert him in his hour of trial. Although Jesus had repeatedly predicted his death, the twelve had not yet been able to integrate such a tragic event into their theology.

For the first and only time in Mark's passion story, Jesus explicitly quotes an OT passage to underscore what he has just predicted, even though there are allusions to OT passages all through the narrative. He quotes Zechariah 13:7, where God commands that the shepherd be struck down, so that the sheep be scattered. In Zechariah that passage is associated with the opening up of a fountain for the cleansing from sin on behalf of the house of David and Jerusalem (Zech 13:1). Here Jesus applies this OT passage to himself. God will strike him, the Shepherd, and the sheep, his disciples, will be scattered. But just as in Zechariah, where the scattering of the sheep leads ultimately to redemption, so also in the case of Jesus and his followers. And that is made clear in the next verse.

B. The Resurrection of Jesus (v. 28). "But after I am raised up, I will go before you to Galilee." After the failure of the disciples to follow Jesus through thick and thin, there is hope beyond Jesus' death: his resurrection. Christ's resurrection will bring them together again in Galilee. He will "go before" them. They will be restored and renewed. This promise is repeated at the end of Mark's Gospel, where the angel at the empty tomb instructs the women to go and tell Jesus' disciples, that he will precede them to Galilee and there they will see him (16:7). The gathering of the church, "the little flock," takes place after Easter; the church is a post-resurrection reality.

Peter evidently heard only half of what Jesus had just said. He was upset when Jesus spoke of the smiting of the shepherd and the scattering of the sheep. Apparently he did not capture the triumphant note in Jesus' prediction of his resurrection from the dead. In any case, as on an earlier occasion, the prediction of a failure in his disciples' loyalty to their Master in the coming hour of trial, called for a protest by Peter.

C. The Denial of Peter (vv. 29-31). "Peter said to him, 'Even though all become deserters, I will not.' Jesus said to him, 'Truly I tell you, this day, this very night, before the cock crows twice, you will deny me three times.' But he said vehemently, 'Even though I must die with you, I will not deny you.' And all of them said the same."

Peter insisted that even if all the other disciples should fail in their loyalty to Jesus, lose faith in him, fall away and be scattered, he would be at least one exception. His explosive rejection of Jesus' prediction indicates how deeply he was offended by the words of Jesus. Boldly he claims that he will remain loyal to Jesus even until death. By challenging Jesus' prophecy, he not only set himself off from his Master, but he also set himself off from the rest of the apostolic band. Others might fail, but not he.

Jesus then responds in the most emphatic manner, with his last Amen- formula found in Mark's Gospel. In the very night, that was already half gone, Peter will deny his Lord three times before the cock crows twice. To deny him three times is idiomatic for denying him totally, completely, thoroughly. Just to give another example of this idiom: Paul prayed three times that God would remove the thorn from his flesh (2 Cor 12:8). To deny means that he will disassociate himself from Jesus; he will desert him, will fall away, will lose faith in him — something Peter said he would never do.

"Cock crow" was a proverbial expression for early morning. The third of the four Roman night watches was designated "cock crow." It has been suggested that Jesus had the bugle signal at the change of the guard in mind when he spoke of the crowing of the cock, but it was not at all uncommon for people in those days to mark time by the more or less regular crowing of roosters.

Although Peter is singled out as the one who vehemently objected to Jesus' prediction of the failure of the disciples to remain true to him, we should not overlook Mark's comment at the end of verse 31, "And all of them said the same." They meant well, but they were not sufficiently aware of their own weakness and vulnerability. And we are reminded of Paul's warning to the self-confident Corinthians, "So if you think you are standing, watch out that you do not fall" (1 Cor 10:12). And that is an admonition we must all take to heart.

Chapter 4

Gethsemane Mark 14:32-42

Holman Hunt, a 19th century English artist, in his painting, The Shadow of the Cross depicts Jesus in his carpenter shop of Nazareth. It's the close of the day and the last rays of the sun are streaming into his shop through the open door. The young carpenter is still toiling at his bench, but then raises himself up from his stooped position and stretches out his arms. Just then the dying sun casts the shadow of his body on the wall behind him, and that shadow is in the form of a cross.

It was the artist's way of reminding us, that the shadow of the cross fell on Jesus' pathway all through his life. But now the hour has come that the Son of Man is to be given over into the hands of sinners, and we want to follow Jesus on his way to Gethsemane. It was in the garden of Gethsemane that Jesus faced the supreme test of whether or not he would go the path of obedience to the Father—a path that would lead ultimately to the cross.

Mark's account of the Last Supper ends with the observation that Jesus and his disciples went out to the Mount of Olives. Passover night had to be spent within the city of Jerusalem, and the Mount of Olives was included in the confines of the city during Passover season. Repeatedly our Lord had said that his hour had not yet come, but now it has come.

Gethsemane presents us with some of the deepest mysteries

of Christ's life. One almost hesitates to analyze this passage, for fear that one might spoil a thing of exquisite beauty and profound mystery. It's almost like picking petals off a flower and thereby spoiling the flower.

However, all scripture is inspired of God, and has been given to us for our learning and for training in righteousness, as Paul puts it. Let us begin, then, with this hallowed place where Jesus wrestled in prayer. Christian tourists today always go to Gethsemane, when they visit Jerusalem, and I have been there myself. The early church did not make much of this sacred place. They did, however, make much of Jesus' prayers and of his solemn sayings in Gethsemane.

I. THE GARDEN OF GETHSEMANE

A. The Place (v. 32a). "They went to a place called Gethsemane." The word "Gethsemane" means "the oil press." The fourth century scholar, Jerome, who gave the church a Latin translation of the Bible, called the Vulgate, followed a different spelling of the word "Gethsemane," and suggested that the word meant "valley of fatness," but that spelling is not generally accepted.

The Gospel of John gives us the added information, that Gethsemane was a garden. There was little space for gardens on Mount Zion, on which the city of Jerusalem lay, and so the more well-to-do had their gardens on the slopes of the Mount of Olives. Jesus and his disciples crossed the ravine, through which the winter-torrent, called Kidron, flowed, and began to ascend the Mount of Olives. Some nameless friend, very likely, had given Jesus permission to use his garden.

There has been a temptation on the part of some interpreters, to connect this garden with the garden of Eden, in which the great tragedy of Adam's fall into sin occurred, but there is little in the text to encourage such a connection. However, the words which Jesus spoke in the garden, do seem to remind us of what happened in the garden of Eden when Adam and Eve sinned. The Fourth Gospel gives us another bit of information with respect to the garden, namely, that Jesus often met there with his disciples (18:2). I suppose that's a reference to former visits to Jerusalem, as well as to the nights he spent there prior to Passover (Lk 21:37). No doubt Judas knew about this place, and after he left the Passover table in the upper room, he went to the authorities to tell them where they could capture Jesus without causing a city-wide ruckus. Mark doesn't call Gethsemane a garden. He says simply, "they came to the plot of land called Gethsemane."

B. The Disciples (vv. 32b,33a). "And he said to his disciples, 'Sit here while I pray'. He took with him Peter and James and John."

Mark has three references in his Gospel to Jesus at prayer. Once at the beginning of his Gospel (1:35), then roughly in the middle (6:46), and here toward the end of the Gospel (14:32). What is interesting is that in all three instances it is night, and in all three he prays alone. We can be sure, that he prayed at other times as well, but Mark singles out these three occurrences.

Here he takes three of his disciples along as witnesses to his prayer and his agony, so that they might be in a position to pass this information on later to the church. After telling the twelve to be seated, he asks Peter, James and John to come with him a little farther. The language has reminded Bible readers of the words of Abraham to his servants, "Sit here... while I and the boy go on farther" (Gen 22:5). But that is simply a literary parallel.

These three apostles had been singled out on several former occasions. They were present when the daughter of Jairus was raised from the dead; they were with Jesus on the Mount of Transfiguration; and here he takes them with him a little farther than the other disciples. Some have interpreted this action of Jesus as favoritism, but that's not the right approach. When

Jesus bestows special privileges, that always means also greater responsibilities. These were to be the leaders of the apostolic band and were to become leaders of the early church.

But there may be another reason why Jesus singled out these three on this occasion. Peter had just claimed that he was ready to die with Jesus, rather than deny him. And James and John had at an earlier occasion (10:35,38), when Jesus had asked them whether they could drink the cup, claimed they could. Now these three are to learn how weak and vulnerable they really were.

Interestingly, there are parallels between the experience of these three disciples on the Mount of Transfiguration and in Gethsemane. Jesus took Peter, James and John to the mountain and there God revealed his Son to them. They heard the words from heaven: 'You are my beloved Son" (9:7). By contrast, here in Gethsemane the Son reveals God as Father. Jesus prays, "Abba, Father." Also, in Mark 9:6 it is said, that Peter did not know what he was saying, and here we read (v. 40), "their eyes were burdened, and they did not know what they should answer him."

So Jesus leaves the twelve behind, takes Peter, James and John with him, and then goes to pray alone. The most significant decisions of our lives, also, must often be made in the deep loneliness of our souls, and so it was with Jesus in Gethsemane.

The account of Jesus' struggle in Gethsemane probably came from these three disciples, close enough to Jesus to hear his cries, for it is hard to conceive of all three of them falling asleep promptly when Jesus left them and went to pray alone. The account certainly bears the marks of historicity, for no one in the early church would have invented a story such as this — a story that is so damaging to the leading apostles' reputation. While the Savior wrestles with the drinking of the cup of God's wrath, they sleep.

II. THE SORROW OF JESUS

A. His Distress (vv. 33b,34a). "And he began to be distressed and agitated. And he said to them, 'I am deeply grieved, even to death'." In the NT only Mark uses this particular verb for "distressed," "distraught" (***ekthambeomai***). The second verb (***ademoneo***) is found only here and once more in Philippians 2:26 in the NT. It has an interesting etymology. It is derived from the words "not" and ***demos*** which means "home." The German word ***unheimlich*** (fearful because of the strangeness of the situation) does it quite well. Jesus was filled with anguish, horror; he was deeply troubled. The closest parallel probably is Psalm 55:5,6, "My heart was disturbed within me; and the horror of death fell upon me; fear and trembling came upon me, and terror covered me."

Not only does Mark describe Jesus' deep sorrow; he also quotes Jesus, who said to his disciples, "I am deeply grieved even unto death." Jesus' words echo Psalm 42:6, where we have exactly the same wording in the Septuagint version, "Why are you so sorrowful (***perilupos***) my soul?" How are we to interpret these words: "Sorrowful unto death?"

(a) Some think he is simply experiencing such severe inner pain that it makes him think of death. "I feel as if I'm dying," we might say.

b) Another way of reading these words might be: "My sorrow is so great it's killing me." It's bringing me to the brink of death.

(c) Still others have understood Jesus to say, "My sorrow is so great, I wish I could die." That would be like Elijah saying, "It's enough, take away my life."

However this last interpretation seems entirely out of context. Jesus is not expressing a longing for death. In a moment we will hear him ask the Father, to let this cup pass by. And so it is better to think of Jesus as feeling the terrors of death.

Jesus' agony in Gethsemane, as he faces death on the cross,

indicates how strong the temptation of the devil must have been, when at the beginning of Jesus' ministry, the evil one tried to persuade him not to go the path of suffering and death, but to choose the path of earthly honor and greatness. It also explains why Jesus spoke so harshly to Peter, when he tried to deter him from going the way of the cross. "Get behind me Satan," he said.

B. His Request (v. 34b). "Remain here and watch." These words evidently were spoken to the three leading apostles. "Remain here" matches the command "sit here" (v. 32), which was given to all the disciples. But what did Jesus mean when he exhorted them "to keep on watching?"

(a) One suggestion is that Jesus had the Passover nightwatch in mind. In Exodus 12:42 God through Moses instructs his people, that they are to keep a watch on this night for all generations. But, after eating the Passover, and after instituting the Lord's Supper, Mark doesn't seem to have any further interest in the Jewish Passover celebrations.

(b) Perhaps it meant to stay physically and mentally awake, so as to witness Jesus' prayer and suffering.

(c) Another view is that they were to keep watch, so that they not be caught in a surprise attack. But when one remembers that Jesus discouraged resistance, this is not likely.

(d) Perhaps it meant that they should stand by him, stay awake as a companionable gesture, so that he would not be utterly alone as he wrestled with the drinking of the cup.

(e) However, the exhortation to watch may also be another way of saying what Peter writes in his first epistle: "Be sober and watch, for your adversary the devil as a roaring lion walks about seeking whom he might devour" (5:8). In verse 38 the exhortation to watch and pray is given in the light of the danger of succumbing to temptation.

And with that we come to the prayer of Jesus.

III. THE PRAYER OF JESUS

"And going a little farther, he threw himself on the ground and prayed that, if it were possible, the hour might pass from him. He said 'Abba, Father, for you all things are possible; remove this cup from me; yet, not what I want, but what you want'" (vv. 35,36). Mark gives us this prayer in two forms. In verse 35 we have it in indirect discourse, and in verse 36 we have direct discourse, i.e., the actual prayer of Jesus. And what did Jesus ask for?

A. That the Hour Might Pass From Him (v. 35). Jesus now leaves the three leading disciples behind and goes a little farther. Luke says "a stone's throw." Not so far away that they couldn't see or hear him. And then he falls on the ground, i.e., on his knees with his face touching the ground. Mark has the imperfect tense, which in Greek is used for continuous or repeated action. We should think of Jesus as falling on his face again and again. Other postures in prayer were also known in Judaism, such as standing, but falling on one's knees and face indicates great seriousness.

Mark says, Jesus prayed, "if possible;" God should let this hour pass from him. We have at least three occasions in Mark in which Jesus predicted his death as God's plan for him (8:31; 9:31; 10:33,34). And now he prays that if possible the hour might pass from him. This has often puzzled interpreters, and various attempts have been made to solve this problem.

(a) One explanation goes like this: Jesus did not really ask, that God should change his mind about his impending death, but rather that he was afraid he might die in Gethsemane before he reached the cross.

(b) Another line of thought is this: Jesus wanted the hour in Gethsemane to pass away as quickly as possible, so that his agony not be prolonged, not that he was asking God to change his plan.

(c) But there is nothing wrong with asking God to change his mind. We have good OT precedent for that. Moses asked God to change his mind when God was about to destroy Israel, after they had worshiped the golden bull-calf. Moses implored God, "O Lord, turn from your fierce wrath; change your mind and do not bring disaster upon this people" (Ex 32:11,12). Or, take Hezekiah, who is told that he will die. He then prays fervently to God to change his mind, and the prophet Isaiah informs Hezekiah, that God will heal him (2 Kgs 20).

Such prayers are not signs of rebellion against God, but they are expressions of confidence in God's love and justice. God will listen to the prayer and, if it is compatible with his providence, will grant the request. In 2 Samuel 15:25,26, David, who had been forced to leave Jerusalem and flee across the Kidron Valley, asks Zadok to go back to Jerusalem with the ark, symbolizing David's prayer, in the hope that God might let him come back. But David adds, "Let him deal with me as he likes." That's a parallel to Jesus' prayer in Gethsemane. When Jesus says "if possible," he is not suggesting that God's power is limited, but rather, if it can be reconciled with God's plan, that he should die on a cross, the hour should pass.

The "hour" which Jesus asks the Father to let pass, is the great moment in salvation history when Christ will taste death for every human being; it is the hour in which Christ will break the power of sin; it is the hour in which Christ will procure our redemption by his substitutionary death on the cross.

Repeatedly in the Gospel of John Jesus says, "My hour has not yet come." But now it was there. The word "hour" is not simply a reference to time. It is an hour of human history, determined by God, loaded with deep significance. It was the turning point of the ages. And the abbreviations B.C. and A.D. are not merely helpful ways of marking time in history; they are confessions of Christian faith. That's why Jewish writers will not use A.D., for that means "the year of our Lord." They prefer to use C.E., meaning "the common era." In our passage this "hour" seems to be used synonymously with the word "cup," which we have in v. 36. First he prays that the hour might pass away, and then he prays that the cup be taken from him.

        B. That the Cup Be Taken From Him (v. 36). The word "cup" is used metaphorically in our text, as often in the OT. Although it can be the symbol of joy, as in Psalm 23, "my cup overflows," it is more often a symbol of suffering, even of God's wrath.

In Mark 10:38,39 Jesus asks James and John, who wanted to sit at his right and left in the kingdom, whether they are able to drink the cup which Jesus would drink, and they claimed they were able. In that passage it clearly refers to Christ's death, but hardly to suffering the wrath of God for the sins of the world. That was something James and John could not do.

The cup in our passage must refer to Christ's substitutionary, atoning death on the cross. And to shudder at the prospect of such a cruel fate, would then be another pointer to Jesus' humanity. Although there have been people, like Socrates, who seemingly died stoically without wavering, Jesus' death is of a different order. Our Lord was facing the hour when he would bear the sins of the world "on his body to the tree". Of that meaning of the word "cup" we as mortal human beings know nothing. Only a God-man understood what that meant.

In his prayer to let the cup pass by, Jesus addresses God as "Abba." No doubt he always did that when he prayed, but this is the only place in the Gospels where this Aramaic word for "Father" is found. Mark translates it for his Greek readers, suggesting, no doubt, that when believers pray to God, they should also address him in this way. "Abba" reflects the bilingualism of the Palestinian church. Paul uses it twice in his letters (Rom 8:15 and Gal 4:6). In Jewish literature there is no reference to this rather intimate way of speaking to God in prayer. We might add, that the word "Abba" is a caritative, an endearment word, meaning "dear Father."

"God is in heaven and you are on earth," said the rabbis, and so one should not address God too intimately. In fact it was custom to use substitutes for God, such as "heaven," "the power," "the highest," the name," etc. To be sure, God is known as Father in the OT, but there it is used with reference to God as the Creator of all things, and also as the one who creates a people for himself, namely, Israel. Israel is his son; he is Israel's Father. The prophet Malachi asks: "Do we not all have one Father? Has not one God created us?" (2:10) But, for an individual to claim that God is his or her Father, is something new. Jesus, however, knew God as his Father, and it is not without significance that Abba is found only here in the Gospels, where Jesus faces God-forsakenness on the cross. And that is instructive for us as believers: as long as we can say "Abba", we need not despair, even though we cannot explain some of the mysteries and enigmas of life.

His prayer, that God should let the cup pass by, is preceded with the confident confession, "all things are possible" for God. This prayer, however, has a very important addendum: "not what I will, but what you will." There are parallels between this prayer and the prayer which our Lord taught us, his disciples, to pray. It too begins with "Father," and in it Jesus teaches us to pray, "Let your will be done on earth, as it is in heaven." Moreover, it also has the petition, "Do not lead us into temptation," and here in verse 38, Jesus exhorts his disciples to watch and pray lest they fall into temptation.

If Jesus is our model in the way we address God, namely as Abba, we should not overlook what Jesus adds to his request: "Not my will but yours be done." Christian believers from earliest times have imitated Jesus in expressing their submission to God's will when they prayed. For example, from Acts 21:14 we learn, that when Paul's friends tried to dissuade him from going to Jerusalem, he finally said, "Let the will of the Lord be done." And the apostle James exhorts his readers to say, as they make their plans, "if the Lord wills, we will live and do this or that" (4:15). In former generations people often added the abbreviation D.V. when they spoke of their plans and intentions. That's Latin for ***Deo volente,*** if the Lord wills. Even if we don't write it, we should always carry this attitude in our hearts.

This prayer of Jesus, to let the cup pass by, and the expression of complete submission to the will of the Father, was repeated three times. In verse 41 we are told that he came for the third time and found them asleep.

IV. THE WEAKNESS OF THE DISCIPLES

A. Their Physical Weakness (v. 37). "And he came and found them sleeping; and he said to Peter, 'Simon, are you asleep? Could you not keep awake one hour? Keep awake and pray that you may not come into temptation; the spirit is willing, but the flesh is weak.'"

Because Jesus addresses Simon Peter personally, we may assume that the observation, that he found "them" sleeping, refers specifically to the three whom he had taken with him a little further. However, by the end of our passage, he seems to have all the disciples in mind. Peter had claimed that he was willing to suffer martyrdom for his Lord, but now he could not even keep his eyes open for an hour. Luke, in his Gospel, shields the disciples by adding, that they were worn out by grief. And because of their physical weakness, Jesus warns them against the spiritual danger that lurks around the comer.

B. The Spiritual Danger (v. 38). He exhorts them to "watch and pray." These words are probably what is called a hendiadys, i.e., two words used to express the same idea. Failure to watch and pray would set them up for a test, which they would not be able to pass—temptation to fall away, to deny their Lord. In fact, that's what happened.

The coming hour will turn out to be dangerous for them, and this all the more because of the weakness of the flesh. "The spirit is willing but the flesh is weak." That antithesis has been understood in more than one way:

(a) Some read the Pauline conflict between flesh and Spirit into this saying. In Paul, "flesh" usually stands for the evil power that has invaded our lives, and "Spirit" is the Holy Spirit, the Spirit of God. These two, Paul explains, are at war with one another.

(b) However, there is good evidence from Semitic backgrounds that flesh and spirit are the human being considered under two different aspects. Flesh represents the tangible, perishable, earthly aspect. It connotes weakness, but not necessarily sinfulness, as it usually does in Paul. And "spirit" in that case is the human spirit through which people can be moved to do that which pleases God. There may be a reference here to the "willing spirit" mentioned in Psalm 51:12. Flesh represents the vulnerability of the human being; it is what Satan uses to distract people from doing what pleases God.

For Christian readers this is a word of comfort ("the flesh is weak"). It assures us that Jesus takes our human frailty into account. He remembers that we are dust, as the Psalmist puts it. He also knows that the deep desires of our spirit are often not fulfilled because of the limitations of our humanity. And so we must remain modest in our claims to spiritual attainments, never forgetting, that sometimes just at the high points of our spiritual experiences we are in danger of falling into sin. And with that we come to our final point.

V. THE COMING OF THE HOUR

"And he went away and prayed, saying the same words. And once more he came and found them sleeping, for their eyes were very heavy; and they did not know what to say to him. He came for the third time and said to them, 'Are you still sleeping and taking your rest? Enough! The hour has come; the Son of Man is betrayed into the hands of sinners. Get up, let us be going. See, my betrayer is at hand'" (vv. 39-42).

Jesus had cried to God three times. To do something three times meant to do it thoroughly. Peter later denies Christ three times. After the resurrection Jesus asked him three times whether he loved him, and then gave him his commission. To pray three times that the cup should pass away should, however, not be understood as a kind of resistance to the Father's will on the part of Jesus. He was willing all along to go the path of obedience, and after praying three times, he was sure that it was the Father's will that he should give his life for the sins of the world. According to Luke, an angel came and strengthened him. And so with a deep inner peace our Lord will now go forth to do the Father's will.

Not only did he put his request to the Father three times, but he also said three times, "Not my will be yours be done." In the garden of Eden, Adam, the head of the human race had in effect said, "Not your will but mine be done," and lost paradise as a result. The last Adam, Jesus, said the opposite, "Your will, not mine, be done," and thereby opened the gates of paradise for our lost and fallen race.

But what did Jesus mean when he asked his disciples, "Are you still sleeping and resting?"

(a) Not all translations put that in question form. If it is a question then it looks as if Jesus expresses his disappointment at the failure of his disciples to watch and pray with him.

(b) The verbs could also be read as a statement: "What, you are sleeping and resting." That would also be an expression of disappointment.

(c) But the verbs have exactly the same form in the imperative mood, and so we could say, "Sleep on now; have your rest." In other words Jesus gave up on them. All of these renderings make sense, and a translator must decide which of these options he thinks best.

We have an even greater translation problem with the word "enough" (*apechei* in Greek). It can mean to receive in full or to hinder or to be far away, and so forth, and the translator must decide which rendering fits the context best.

(a) One suggestion is that Jesus had the meaning "received in full," in mind. Judas had received the sum of money promised him for betraying Jesus. The bargain had been completed and the machinery set in motion to have Jesus arrested. That hour has now come, let's be up and going. Judas had left the Passover table after he found out where Jesus planned to spend the night, and he would soon be there to capture the One who had called him several years earlier to be his disciple.

(b) However, Jesus may have meant "enough of sleeping and resting," the hour has now come. The Son of Man is being betrayed or given over into the hands of sinners. To be given over into the "hands of sinners" is Semitic for being given over into their power. Jesus began his ministry with the message that he had come to call sinners to repentance (Mk 2:17), and now in the end he is given over into the power of sinful men. The expression "to give over" plays an important role in the Passion story. It has a double meaning, for it also means "to betray."

Judas gives Jesus over to the chief priests, he betrays him; the chief priests give him over to Pilate; Pilate gives him over to the soldiers to be crucified. But there is another perspective. He was given over by God. "This man," said Peter in his Pentecost sermon, "was given over to you according to the definite plan and foreknowledge of God" (Acts 2:23). Paul writes to the Romans, that God spared not his only Son, but gave him over for us all" (Rom 8:32).

This expression has a background in Isaiah 53, where it is said of the suffering servant, that God gave him over for our sins (v. 6). So the "giving over" suggests that Jesus death was in the plan of God. On the other hand, it also describes the sinister action on the part of Judas, who betrayed the Son of

Man. Our passage ends with Jesus' exhortation, "Get up; let us go!"

Although the disciples had failed to watch and pray, and although Jesus knows that they are not ready to pass the test that awaits them, and although he had predicted that on this night they would all forsake him, he hasn't given up on them. He still wants them to go with him to encounter the traitor together. They will not stand firm in the hour of testing, but they are on his side. Weak they may be, but they are not on the side of the sinners into whose hands he will be given over. And so, through the lines of our story, in which Jesus expresses deep disappointment in his disciples, because they could not watch for even an hour, there shines the grace of God that calls people who are beset by the weaknesses of the flesh, to come with him. And that call comes to us even today.

The Jewish scholar Montefiore says of this story, "One cannot but marvel at the wonderful grace and beauty, the exquisite tact and discretion which the narrative displays; there is not a word too little; there is not a word too much."

Chapter 5

The Betrayal and Arrest of Jesus Mark 14:23-52

In the garden of Gethsemane Jesus had made his great decision: he would do the Father's will; he would take the road to Calvary; he would be obedient unto death. There was now no turning back; the hour for which he had come into the world had finally arrived, and he would not flinch. In perfect trust he would subject his body to torture and a cruel death, bearing our sins on his body to the cross, as Peter puts it in his first epistle (2:24), so that we might be free from the power of sin and eternal death.

No sooner had Jesus come to this great decision, when the quiet of the garden was broken with trampling feet, the clanking of arms and the shouting of men. His enemies were not going to take any chances and had assembled a sizable squad of armed men, to make sure that this time Jesus was not going to slip away on them. They were not out to arrest Jesus' disciples, for they were convinced, that if they captured their leader, his followers would disintegrate.

Today we want to focus on this tragic account of Jesus' betrayal and arrest in Gethsemane, as found in Mark's Gospel. The other Gospels contribute some interesting details not found in Mark and we will try to weave some of them into our study. We begin with a look at the arresting party.

I. THE ARRESTING PARTY

A. The Leader of the Party (v. 43a). "Immediately, while he was still speaking, Judas, one of the twelve, arrived; and with him there was a crowd with swords and clubs, from the chief priests, the scribes, and the elders."

Chapter 14 of Mark's Gospel begins with the report that the Jewish authorities had made the decision that Jesus must be put to death. They knew that they would have to engage in stealthy maneuvers if they were to carry out this plan without creating a riot during the festival.

Shortly thereafter, we are told in verses 10 and 11, that Judas Iscariot, one of the twelve, went to the chief priests to arrange for Jesus' arrest. The chief priests are overjoyed at the offer and promise to give him money. We next meet Judas at the Passover table (vv. 18-21) where Jesus tells him that it would be better not to be born than to betray the Son of Man. At that point Mark drops the curtain on Judas, but according to John's Gospel, Judas slipped away after the meal "and it was night" (Jo 13:30). The literal darkness into which Judas disappeared, after he had made the wretched choice to betray his Master, was probably symbolic of the spiritual darkness which now entered his soul.

Judas's fellow disciples were not fully conscious of the evil machinations that were going on behind the scenes. In fact they thought, when Judas left the Passover table, he was going to buy what they needed for the festival of unleavened bread and, also, to give something to the poor—a standard practice at Passover. We know that Judas was the treasurer of the apostolic band and it was only natural for them to think along these lines. However, they were wrong. He had gone to the Jewish authorities to tell them where they could arrest and capture Jesus.

While Jesus was still speaking to his disciples, after wrestling in prayer in the garden of Gethsemane, "Judas, one of the Twelve, arrived." Precisely what Jesus was saying to his disciples when he was interrupted with the arrival of Judas is not stated, but if we look closely at the end of the previous passage, Jesus tells them to get up for his betrayer is at hand (v. 42).

All three Synoptic Gospels open the scene of Jesus' arrest with the comment that Judas was one of the Twelve. There seems to be a note of sorrow in that comment. Mark and his fellow Evangelists must have found it hard to write those words. It seemed so incredible, that one of their own should have sunk to such depths of wickedness. They make no attempt to blacken his character; they don't call him opprobrious names. They simply report the sad story of how he betrayed Jesus.

Our passage pictures him as the leader of the arresting party. After the resurrection of Jesus, Judas was replaced by Matthias, in order to fill in the gap that Judas had left. In Luke's account of that event, Peter tells Christ's followers that Judas had been "a guide of those of those who arrested Jesus" (Acts 1:16). And that's the picture we get of Judas in the opening words of our text. Judas knew where Jesus had intended to spend Passover night and had gone to the Jewish authorities and offered to show them where they could find Jesus. With him, we are told, was a crowd, and so we need to take a look at this arresting party.

B. The Delegated Crowd (v. 43b). "With him was a crowd with swords and clubs from the high priests, the scribes and the elders." I call this a delegated crowd, because it was authorized and sent by the Sanhedrin. When high priests, scribes and elders are mentioned we can be sure that the Sanhedrin is meant. The Romans had delegated the supervision of Jewish life to this body and, except for festivals, when the Roman army made its presence known in Jerusalem, by and large had turned over responsibility for law and order in the temple city to the Sanhedrin. This body of Jewish rulers had recruited a "crowd" to carry out their evil designs.

This crowd no doubt included members of the temple police

or other servants of the court who were authorized to make arrests even beyond the temple precincts. We know that one of the members of the crowd was a servant of the High Priest. Whether any Roman soldiers were among this arresting party cannot be said with certainty. It should be noted, however, that John, in the Fourth Gospel, speaks of a "cohort"—a word used in the Roman army. If there were any soldiers in this crowd, then Pilate must have received some information on what the Sanhedrin was up to. In any case, we should not think of the arresting part as rabble, recruited from the street.

Although Jesus taught the way of peace and abhorred all violence, this crowd is armed to the teeth. They have swords and wooden clubs, the kind of weapons used both by temple police and Roman authorities. And so the stage is set for Jesus' arrest. This "crowd" sent by the Sanhedrin evidently did not know Jesus, and so Judas, after leading them to the Mount of Olives, identifies him with a kiss.

II. THE KISS OF JUDAS

A. The Prearranged Sign (v. 44). "Now the betrayer had given them a sign, saying, 'The one I will kiss is the man; arrest him and lead him away under guard'." The kiss was a token of homage with which disciples customarily greeted their rabbi, although we never read of the disciples kissing Jesus. Since it was night, and Jesus was surrounded by his disciples, and the crowd did not personally know Jesus, it was important to have someone who knew Jesus well, identify him.

But what did Judas mean when he instructed the arresting party to "arrest him and lead him away under guard?" The Greek *asphalos* can also mean "safely," rather than "under guard." This possible translation has led to speculation that Judas was already sorry for what he had done, and that he had a secret plan whereby Jesus would emerge triumphant, but that is very unlikely. Judas was not interested in the safety of Jesus, but in his not getting away. The tragedy is, that a man who had lived so close to Jesus for three years could so steel his heart against his Master. His main concern now was, that the arrest should go smoothly before morning dawned.

B. The Judas Kiss (v. 45). "So when he came, he went up to him at once and said, 'Rabbi!' and kissed him." What makes this action of Judas so awful is that he kissed Jesus so affectionately. In verse 44 we have the simple verb *phileo* for kiss, but in verse 45 we have the compound *kataphileo* meaning that he kissed him again and again or that he kissed him tenderly. By choosing this word Mark seems to heighten the tragedy of what was happening here. In his desire to make sure that the Master would be recognized, Judas was unusually demonstrative in his display of affection. To this day the "Judas kiss" stands for betrayal under the guise of friendship.

Judas follows up his kiss with the familiar address: "Rabbi!" There was nothing unusual about students addressing their teacher in this way; although Jesus had reservations about it (Mt 23:7,8). At the last supper the other disciples ask, "Is it I Lord?" but Judas uses "Rabbi" (Mt 26:25). That may have been an indication that he was already outside the company of Jesus' disciples.

Mark leaves Judas's greeting and kiss unanswered by Jesus. In Matthew, however, Jesus responds with, "Friend, why have you come?" (26:50). Here we face a translation problem, for this may be a statement rather a question. For that reason the NIV has, "Friend, do what you came for," and the NEB has, "Friend, do what you are here to do." In any case, these were the grieved words of the Lord in response to base treachery.

III. THE SEIZURE OF JESUS

A. The Arrest (v. 46). "Then they laid hands on him and arrested him." Jesus offered no resistance when the arresting party laid hands on him. Whether they gave Jesus the reason for arresting him is not stated. A series of charges were brought against Jesus at his trial, but no reasons are given in the accounts of his arrest. To "lay hands" on someone often meant, to do the person harm (cf. LXX Gen 22:12; 2 Sam 18:12). In our passage it means physical seizure, but with overtones of hostile intent. What happened after they had arrested Jesus, according to Mark, becomes plain in verse 53, where it is said that "they took Jesus to the high priest; and all the high priests, the elders, and the scribes were assembled." Mark's report on Jesus' arrest is extremely brief and succinct. Other Gospels include numerous details of what happened between the moment when Jesus was seized and when he was led away to his trial. One incident that is reported by all four Gospels is Peter's attempt to defend his Master with a sword.

B. The Defence (v. 47). "But one of those who stood near drew his sword and struck the slave of the high priest, cutting off his ear."

For reasons not given to us by Mark, the name of the disciple who drew his sword is not mentioned. But the apostle John not only tells us that it was Simon Peter who struck the slave of the high priest, but he also gives us the name of this servant, namely Malchus (Jo 18:10). Perhaps when the Fourth Gospel was written (toward the end of the first century) it was safe to mention these men by name. Malchus may have been sent by the high priest with the arresting party in order to bring back a full report on what had happened. Whether Peter had singled him out or whether he happened to be at the wrong place when Peter unsheathed his sword, is not certain.

This was an impulsive reaction on the part of Peter and ran counter to what Jesus had taught. Later, when our Lord stood before Pilate, he made it very clear, that if his kingdom were of this world, then his disciples would fight (Jo 18:36). But the kingdom of God must not be defended or extended by violence. Peter very likely had aimed at the head but got only the ear.

In fact Mark has the diminutive of "ear" (***otarion***), leading some scholars to suggest that he got only the earlobe. Luke, the physician, reports that it was the "right ear." Peter had misunderstood the conversation about the two swords, reported in Luke's Gospel (22:35-38).

Jesus, in his warning about the impending crisis that his disciples would face that night, counselled them to take purse and bag and sword. It was his way of concretizing readiness for the coming contingency when he would be captured and tried. When the disciples responded with, "Lord, look, here are two swords," Jesus knew they had misunderstood him and said, "enough of that." It wasn't the first time that the disciples had misunderstood Jesus. He was not suggesting that they should arm themselves and attack his captors with swords. Rather he wanted them to be spiritually and morally prepared for the hour when Jesus would be apprehended, when their loyalty to the Master would be put to the test.

That Jesus did not endorse Peter's action can be gathered from the fact that the other Gospels report, that Jesus rebuked Peter, and Luke reports that he healed the ear of the servant. Some scholars think that if Jesus had not healed the ear of Malchus, he might have been accused of violence when he appeared before the governor. Malchus may have become a Christian, otherwise his name would probably not have been retained in the gospel.

Jesus had exhorted Peter to watch and pray with him, lest he enter into temptation. But Peter passed the time sleeping and was not prepared for this moment. Although he was wrong in the manner in which he defended his Master, we have to give him credit for his devotion to Jesus. He meant well, but he had not yet understood what Jesus had said repeatedly about his coming sufferings and death.

This is the kind of mistake that has been made over and over again in Christian history. Zealous souls, out of love for Christ, have done things which embarrassed the Christian church. Wars have been waged in the name of Christ. Crusades have been mounted in his name. State-churches have persecuted both Christians and Jews under the banner of Christ.

Interestingly, Peter was not apprehended for his rash act. Perhaps the arresting party was so sure, that the followers of Jesus would disintegrate once their Master was captured, that they couldn't be bothered with what seemed to them a trifle. Moreover, Jesus healed the servant's ear. He was true to his own words: "Love your enemies, do good to those who hate you" (Lk 6:27). Jesus then expresses surprise that the arresting party has come armed to the teeth to seize him. But he sees this entire event as a fulfillment of Scripture.

IV. THE FULFILMENT OF SCRIPTURE

"Then Jesus said to them, 'Have you come out with swords and clubs to arrest me as though I were a bandit? Day after day I was with you in the temple teaching, and you did not arrest me. But let the scriptures by fulfilled'" (vv. 48,49).

Mark does not mention the fact that Jesus rebuked Peter for his impulsive action. Rather, he addresses the arresting party and expressed his indignation at the unusual show of force mustered against him, as if he were an armed robber. Surely there was no need to be armed with swords and clubs in order to capture someone who had made himself completely vulnerable as he taught in the temple. This rebuke must have stung his captors, for they knew that the Jewish hierarchy would have been only too happy to arrest him earlier, but they feared the crowds would riot.

But what did Jesus mean when he said, "Let the scriptures be fulfilled?" On the one hand, we are reminded of the Suffering Servant of Isaiah, of whom it was said that he "was numbered with the transgressors" (Isa 53:12). On the other hand, since the flight of the disciples is mentioned in verse 50, it would be appropriate to recall the words of Zechariah 13:7, which Jesus quoted earlier, when he predicted their flight (Mk 14:27). But Jesus may not have had specific scripture passages in mind when he spoke of the fulfillment of scripture. It may well be that he wanted to say that the OT scriptures as a whole were being fulfilled.

For Christian readers of Mark's Gospel it must have been of some significance, that what happened in the garden of Gethsemane was in keeping with God's plan of salvation. Some may have wondered, why it was, that the One who had raised the dead to life, who had calmed raging storms, who had cast out demons, could not escape this arresting party. But Jesus allowed himself to be captured and mistreated and killed because he was fulfilling God's salvatory purposes.

V. THE FLIGHT OF JESUS' FOLLOWERS

A. The Flight of the Eleven. "All of them deserted him and fled" (v. 50).

By now it was apparent that Jesus was to be taken away by those who had arrested him. He had not made any effort to avoid being captured. In Matthew's Gospel we are told, that when Jesus rebuked Peter for his violent reaction, he explained that he could appeal to his heavenly Father and he would at once send twelve legions of angels to protect him (Mt 26:53), but then the scriptures would not be fulfilled.

When the eleven saw that Jesus did not call on them to defend him, they abandoned him and fled. Jesus had predicted that they would all be offended (Mk 14:27), they would stumble, stagger, trip (***skandalizomai***). Jesus had predicted that one of the twelve would betray him, and that prediction had now been fulfilled. He had also predicted that the disciples would fail in their loyalty to their Master, and that also was being fulfilled when they abandoned Jesus to his fate. A third prediction, namely that Peter would deny him three times, will be fulfilled shortly.

When Jesus called his first disciples, Mark reports that they left their nets and followed him. Of James and John it is said that they even left their father and followed him (1:18; 1:20). And now at the end of their internship they left Jesus. Forsaken by his closest friends, he is now on the Way of Sorrows, that will lead to his atoning death. On the way out of the garden of Gethsemane a young man follows Jesus and his captors. Who could he possibly have been?

B. The Young Man

"A certain young man was following him, wearing nothing but a linen cloth. They caught hold of him, but he left the linen cloth and ran off naked" (vv. 51,52).

Since Mark is the only one of our four Evangelists who records this event, it has often been suggested that the young man was Mark himself. Did Matthew and Luke omit this story out of deference, not wanting to embarrass Mark? (Like the other disciples, this young man also fled when he was threatened with arrest.) It must have been someone who lived nearby and who perhaps was roused out of sleep by the noisy arresting party. We know that Mark lived in Jerusalem where his mother Mary had a house of some size, for it was one of the places where the early Christian church gathered (Acts 12:12).

Some have even gone so far as to suggest that the upper room in which Jesus and his disciples ate the Passover, was in Mary's house, and that Mark followed them when they left after midnight to spend the night in Gethsemane and nearly got caught. That is all a bit speculative, but "to follow Jesus" is the regular way in which his disciples were designated.

But why was he not properly dressed? It looks as if he was roused out of his sleep and quickly threw a linen sheet over himself and hurried to see what was going on. If Jesus and his disciples ate the Passover in the upper room of Mark's family home, then it is possible that Judas and the arresting party came to the house first, to see whether Jesus was still there. When they saw that he had left, they went after him in Gethsemane. Mark then, being awakened, wrapped a sheet around himself and ran to the garden, perhaps to let Jesus know what was about to happen. Or, he may have slipped out of bed when Jesus and the disciples left and followed them, secretly observing what was going on. That's all very intriguing and imaginative, but we don't know for certain who this young man was.

Whoever this young man was, he failed the test of discipleship. He wanted to follow Jesus, but when the crunch came, he fled like the other disciples. He was even willing to flee in disgrace, for to appear without clothes was considered to be a disgrace in Israel. (Although the word "naked" can at times mean simply "scantily clad.") The prophet Amos spoke of a coming day when "the stout of heart among the mighty shall flee away naked" (2:16). If that could happen to the stout of heart, then we should not be so surprised that it happened to this would-be follower of Jesus.

If indeed Mark was this unnamed young man, who fled in shame when his discipleship was put to the test, then perhaps it is Mark's way of telling his readers: I failed in the hour of testing, but by God's grace I was restored and, later, I was called to carry the gospel to "the ends of the earth" (Acts 13:13; 15:39). What an encouragement his story must have been to the readers of Mark's day who were called upon to suffer because of their allegiance to Christ and, what an encouragement it us for us today! The word "young man" (***neaniskos***) is found in Mark only in one other place, namely in the resurrection narrative (Mk 16:5). There a young man sits in the empty tomb, explaining to the women who had come to the tomb, that Jesus was alive. Perhaps Mark wanted to show the contrast between these two young men. The Jesus who had been abandoned so disgracefully by all of his disciples (Joh 16:32), including this young man, and who had been left to face arrest and death all alone, triumphs over death in the end, and a heavenly young man proclaims that he is risen from the dead, never to die again, but to offer eternal life to all who believe in him.

Chapter 6

Jesus' Trial by the Sanhedrin Mark 14:53-65

We have now come to some of the more dramatic scenes in the Passion narrative of Mark's Gospel. Although individual Gospel writers make their unique contribution to the story of Christ's death, they are agreed in the broad outline of this moving account. It is not possible to give an hour by hour timetable of the events that filled that awful night when Christ was captured, his disciples dispersed, and our Lord was arraigned before the Jewish authorities, but the sequence of events is not hard to discern.

According to John's Gospel, Jesus was first taken to Annas before he was put on trial before the Sanhedrin (Jo 18:13). Annas had been high priest some fifteen years before his son-in-law, Caiaphas, took over that position, and was still a powerful figure behind the Sanhedrin. In the fifty years following the deposition of Annas, five of his sons became high priests, as well as a son-in law (Caiaphas) and a grandson. We are not surprised, then, that the crowd that apprehended Jesus on the Mount of Olives took him first to Annas. To meet in the house of Annas for an official interrogation was in itself an irregularity in the Jewish justice system at the time. But there were many more such irregularities in the trials of Jesus. The Jewish leaders had but one aim in mind: to do away with Jesus. Annas, we are told (Jo 18:24), sent Jesus handcuffed to Caiaphas. Because the Synoptic

Gospels omit this trial before Annas, we will also skip it, and continue to follow the Marcan outline of the narrative.

It almost appears as if the Sanhedrin was already in session when Jesus was arrested. Matthew reports that those who arrested Jesus took him to Caiaphas the high priest (26:57). Mark agrees with Matthew. He writes, "They took Jesus to the high priest; and all the chief priests, the elders, and the scribes were assembled" (14:53).

With that brief introduction we turn now to Christ's arraignment before the Sanhedrin.

I. THE ARRAIGNMENT BEFORE THE SANHEDRIN

When it is said that "all" the chief priests, elders and scribes were assembled (v.53), it may simply mean that they were present in sufficient numbers to form a quorum. The Sanhedrin was comprised of seventy members plus the high priest who functioned as chairman. When chief priests, elders and scribes are mentioned together, we can be fairly certain that the Sanhedrin is meant. What isn't so clear is, whether this was a formal or an informal meeting of this ruling body, which had jurisdiction over every Jew. It looks as if the Sanhedrin on this night met in Caiaphas's palace, rather than in the so-called "Hall of Stones" in the temple. Mark doesn't mention the high priest's name but Matthew does. It was actually contrary to legal practice for the Sanhedrin to meet at night. In fact it was an established custom, that this governing body did not meet on important festival days.

In the period following the Maccabean wars, when Israel enjoyed independence of other ruling powers, the Sanhedrin had the authority to impose the death-penalty. But now the Romans were in charge and the Roman governor would have to approve the imposition of the death penalty.

In the Mishnah, which is a collection of Jewish traditions, some of the laws that governed the legal procedures of the

Sanhedrin are spelled out. Generally speaking, the Sanhedrin was to defend those who were arraigned before it, lest an innocent person be condemned. For that reason the testimony of at least two witnesses had to be in complete agreement before the accused could be convicted. But we shall see momentarily (v. 55) that in the case of Jesus all these precautions were thrown to the wind.

As the trial of Jesus got under way, Simon Peter, who had fled with the other disciples, is seen following at a distance. Mark cannot tell the story of Jesus' interrogation and of Peter's denial at the same time, so he brings Peter in at this point, but leaves the story of his denial till later.

II. THE COURAGE AND COWARDICE OF PETER

"Peter had followed him at a distance, right into the courtyard of the high priest; and he was sitting with the guards, warming himself at the fire" (v. 54).

One wonders whether Peter still had hopes of rescuing Christ by force? But it may also be that Peter was so thunderstruck by what had happened, when his Master was captured, that he didn't really know what he was doing. To follow Jesus even at a distance was no doubt dangerous, and so we should probably think of a mixture of courage and cowardice in Peter's action. It was a courageous act to enter into the courtyard of the high priest, even though he behaved in a cowardly manner when challenged on the matter of his relationship to Jesus. To follow Jesus "at a distance" is, of course not an expression of true discipleship.

In the courtyard a fire was burning. Fires served a double purpose: they were for light as well as for warmth. Jerusalem lies nearly 3000 feet above sea level, and spring nights can be cold. And so Peter sat down beside the fire together with the "servants"— probably servants of the high priest, including perhaps members of the arresting party. These people would otherwise have gone home by this time of the night, but the extraordinary meeting of the court called for night duty. To sit "with" Jesus' enemies suggests a breakdown in discipleship. It was also a risky thing to do, because it was Peter who had wounded the high priest's servant in the garden.

Before Mark carries the account of Peter's denial any further, he returns to the interrogation that is going on in another part of the high priest's palace.

III. THE ACCUSATIONS OF THE FALSE WITNESSES

"Now the chief priests and the whole council were looking for testimony against Jesus to put him to death; but they found none. For many gave false testimony against him, and their testimony did not agree. Some stood up and gave false testimony against him, saying, 'We heard him say, I will destroy this temple that is made with hands, and in three days I will build another, not made with hands.' But even on this point their testimony did not agree" (vv. 55-59).

To give false witness was a serious violation of one of the ten commandments. In fact, false witnesses were to be put to death. But here they are called to testify against Jesus. According to Deuteronomy 17:6, judgments were based on the agreement of two or three witnesses. But here there was no agreement. The Sanhedrin clearly was not interested in evidence, but wanted to find a way to condemn Jesus to death.

The witnesses against Jesus come up with a charge that they think might stand up in a Roman court, for the death penalty would have to be approved by the Romans. They could have accused him of breaking the Sabbath, or that he had claimed to have authority to forgive sins, or that he had constantly trampled on the Jewish food laws, but they knew that such accusations would be thrown out by the Roman governor.

And so they make an accusation that they thought might stick, for the Romans guaranteed the inviolability of the temple.

Any violation of the temple was considered a capital offence. Stephen, the first Christian martyr, was stoned to death because he was accused of speaking "against this holy place" (Acts 6:13). Later, Paul was captured in the temple, accused of bringing a Gentile into the court of the temple to which only Jews had access, and they nearly tore him to pieces (Acts 21:28). We can see, then, that the accusation that Jesus had threatened to destroy the temple was very serious. Throughout the Greco-Roman world the destruction or desecration of places of worship was often regarded as a capital offence. But even on this point the witnesses did not agree. No wonder; because Jesus actually never said that he intended to destroy the Jerusalem temple.

According to John 2:19, Jesus had said, "Destroy this temple, and I will raise it up in three days." The Evangelist's interpretation of that statement gives us a clue as to what Jesus meant "He spoke of the temple of his body." That Jesus had predicted the demise of the Jerusalem temple, as a divine judgment, is clear from Mark 13, but he had never said that he would destroy it. Perhaps the witnesses didn't agree in their quotation of Jesus' words, or it may even be, that the high priest thought such a charge was not sufficient to warrant the death sentence.

In the legendary Acts of Pilate we are told, that the Sanhedrin got plenty of evidence in favor of Jesus, but that was not what the hierarchy was looking for. Man after man came forward, so the story goes, saying: "I was a leper and he cleansed me; I was blind and he made me see; I was deaf and he made me able to hear; I was lame and he made me walk; I was paralysed and he gave me back my strength." But those were not the kind of things the Sanhedrin wanted to hear; they wanted condemnatory charges.

Having been unsuccessful with false witnesses, the high priest now decides to break the log-jam by questioning Jesus' claim to Messiahship.

IV. THE CHRISTOLOGICAL QUESTION

"Then the high priest stood up before them and asked Jesus, 'Have you no answer? What is it that they testify against you?' But he was silent and did not answer. Again the high priest asked him, 'Are you the Messiah, the Son of the Blessed One?' Jesus said, 'I am; and you will see the Son of Man seated at the right hand of the Power, and coming with the clouds of heaven'" (vv. 60-62).

The standing up of the high priest marks a turn in the proceedings. To stand up to address the prisoner would give his words greater authority. He confronts Jesus directly in the presence of the Sanhedrin, asking him direct questions, hoping, perhaps, to goad him into incriminating himself. There was an element of majesty in the silence of Jesus. One gets the impression that Jesus was completely resigned to the Father's will, and he knows that denying false accusations would not change anything. In retrospect the apostles saw this silence of Jesus foreshadowed in Isaiah 53:7, where the prophet says of the Suffering Servant, "And despite being afflicted, he does not open his mouth, as a sheep led to the slaughter; and as a lamb before its shearers is without voice, so he opens not his mouth." This silence of Jesus became a model for Christians who later had to suffer for Christ's sake. Peter, in his first epistle, reminds his persecuted readers, that Christ "when he was reviled, did not revile; suffering, he did not threaten; he was giving himself to the One judging justly" (1 Pet 2:23).

To break the impasse, the high priest asks Jesus, whether he is the Christ, the Son of the Blessed One. The word "Christ" (*christos*) means the anointed one, and is the Greek equivalent of the Hebrew "Messiah." To begin with it was a title, but eventually, when attached to the name Jesus, it became a proper name: Jesus Christ. This probably happened when the gospel invaded the Greek-speaking world, in which the word *christos* would not have been readily understood. Speaking in Aramaic, no doubt, the common language of Palestine at the time, the high priest wanted to know whether Jesus thought of himself as Messiah. The high priest must have known that Jesus had accepted the title from others, even though Jesus did not use this title as a self-designation, preferring rather to call himself "Son of Man."

The claim to be an "anointed one" (***christos***) would of and by itself not constitute blasphemy (OT prophets were also called "anointed ones"). However, the claim to be "the son of the Blessed One," would be intolerable blasphemy. "The Blessed One" is a reference to God. It is one of the many substitutes used in Jesus' day for God, whose name people generally were somewhat loath to pronounce too often.

Although Jesus was conscious of being Messiah, he not only refrained from calling himself "the Christ," but also discouraged others from proclaiming him as such. This is sometimes called "the Messianic secret." Jesus contemporaries thought of Messiah as a political leader who would restore Israel to political greatness, and for that reason Jesus may have avoided the use of the title "Messiah." When Simon Peter made his great confession at Caesarea Philippi, "You are the Christ" (Mk 8:30), Jesus acknowledged that this insight had come from God. However, he then went on and told his disciples not to tell anyone.

Prior to the cross and the resurrection, our Lord did not openly speak of himself as Messiah. Following his resurrection, however, when it had become plain that Messiahship involved suffering and death, Jesus spoke of himself freely as the Christ. At the moment he was standing in the shadow of the cross, and in response to the high priest's question, "Are you the Messiah?" Jesus answers unequivocally, "I am." In Matthew and Luke Jesus' answer doesn't appear quite so unambiguous. According to Matthew 26:64 Jesus answered, "You have said so." In other words, "Yes, I am Messiah, but probably not the kind of Messiah you have in mind;"

But Jesus said more: "You shall see the Son of Man seated at the right hand of the Power, and coming with the clouds of heaven" (v. 62b). The language Jesus used comes from Daniel 7:13, where, after the beasts, who represent the passing kingdoms of this world, have had their dominion taken away from them, one like the Son of Man comes with the clouds of glory and he is given an everlasting kingdom.

Jesus had regularly spoken of himself as "Son of Man." Sometimes this Semitic expression was simply a substitute for "I." For example, when Jesus said, "The Son of Man is lord even of the Sabbath" (Mk 2:28), he meant "I am lord of the Sabbath." However, in the majority of the cases in which "Son of Man" occurs in the Gospels, this self-designation of Jesus is connected either with his suffering or with his coming in glory. Again and again Jesus had made it clear that the Son of Man would suffer and die. Now, in response to the high priest's question, he speaks of the Son of Man's coming in glory

After the Son of Man has suffered and died, but before he returns in glory at the end of the age, he will be highly exalted by God. He will be seated at the right hand of "the Power." The high priest had called God "the Blessed One"; Jesus calls him "the Power." That was another of the many substitutes for God common in Judaism at the time of Jesus.

To sit at the right hand of God is language taken from Psalm 110:1. Jesus fuses Daniel 7:13 with Psalm 110:1. After the Son of Man has been exalted to God's right hand, he will come with the clouds of heaven at the end of this age. John writes in Revelation 1:7, "Behold he is coming with the clouds and every eye will see him, even those who pierced him; and all the tribes of the earth will wail on account of him." At the moment Jesus is being falsely accused and humiliated, but he knows that God will justify him. He will raise him from the dead and exalt him to his right hand; he will be enthroned. And his enemies, who are bent on putting him to death, will some day have to face him as Judge, when he returns with the clouds of heaven.

On that day even the Jewish Sanhedrin, that was condemning him to death, would stand before the Judge of all the earth.

Jesus had claimed to be Messiah. That was dangerous, for the court could convert that into a political charge and accuse Jesus of sedition before the Roman governor. The Jews expected Messiah to set up his kingdom and make an end of Roman rule. But there were others who claimed to be Messiahs. In fact, Jesus warned his disciples against such false claims (Mk 13:21,22). That claim by itself could hardly be construed as blasphemy. However when Jesus spoke of his exaltation to the right hand of God, and of his future coming in glory; that was too much for Caiaphas.

V. THE CHARGE OF BLASPHEMY

"Then the high priest tore his clothes and said, 'Why do we still need witnesses? You have heard his blasphemy! What is your decision'? All of them condemned him as deserving death" (vv. 63,64).

The reaction of the high priest who, in his moral blindness, was hardly interested in discussing the meaning of Messiahship with Jesus, was to tear his garments. The tearing of one's garments in earlier times was an expression of grief. For example, Jacob tore his clothes on hearing of the death of his son Joseph. David tore his clothes when he heard of the death of Saul and Jonathan. Even among the Romans this gesture might express grief. However in Israel it also became a symbolical action by which one expressed outrage. And that is the meaning here. Tearing clothes did not mean that all of one's clothes were torn to shreds, but simply that one made a tear in one's outer garment from the neck down.

Caiaphas demonstrated his faithfulness to Jewish law by tearing his garment. Godly people were expected to express outrage when they heard blasphemous language. The high priest tore his garment on behalf of all the other members of the

Sanhedrin, and they all chimed in with his verdict: Jesus is guilty of blasphemy. If that was the case, they did not need any more witnesses; they had what they wanted. There is a tone of triumph in Caiaphas's words, perhaps even of savage glee. He had tried earlier to get Jesus to speak, hoping that he would incriminate himself. But the charges brought against him were false. Later, when he is asked directly: "Are you the Messiah?" Jesus gave a clear and positive answer.

The members of the Sanhedrin all agreed with the high priest, that Jesus was guilty of blasphemy and deserved the death penalty. According to Leviticus 24:16, the punishment for blasphemy was death by stoning. However, since the Romans would have to carry out the death penalty, the charge before Pilate would have to be turned into a political charge. Pilate would hardly be interested in judging someone who, in the eyes of the Jewish authorities, had blasphemed. And so this preliminary court session ended with the formal decision to hand Jesus over to the Roman procurator (Mk 15:1) who, they hoped, would carry out the execution.

Now that the council had condemned Jesus to death, they thought it necessary to show their revulsion at Jesus' claims, and so they subject Jesus to despicable acts of abuse and mockery.

VI. THE ABUSE AND MOCKERY OF JESUS

"Some began to spit on him, to blindfold him, and to strike him, saying to him, 'Prophecy!' The guards also took him over and beat him"(v. 65).

It is not stated who the "some" were who mistreated Jesus. Mark gives us the distinct impression that members of the high court, the Sanhedrin, were involved. They showed their contempt for Jesus in a very opprobrious manner. However, Mark also mentions the servants, attendants, or guards who participated in the mistreatment of Jesus.

They spit in Jesus' face to show their utter contempt for him. After all, Messiah was to be powerful, able to vanquish all his foes. But this would-be Messiah was helpless. How could he possibly be Messiah? Bible readers have seen an OT background for this despicable act of spitting in Jesus' face. In Isaiah 50:6,7 the Suffering Servant says, "I gave my cheeks to slaps; I did not turn my face from the shame of spitting. And the Lord God became my helper, and so I was not ashamed."

Also, they blindfolded him, beat him with fists, and then asked him to "prophesy," meaning, to identity the person who had cuffed him. It is a cruel form of the children's game, known as "blind man's bluff"—a game known even in ancient times. The word "prophesy," which in this context means "identify" was probably used to make fun of Jesus' many prophetic utterances. For example, he predicted the destruction of the temple, which they must have thought was preposterous. According to a Jewish interpretation of Isaiah 11:2-4, where it is stated that the shoot from the stump of Jesse would not judge by what he saw or heard, Messiah was said to be one who could judge by "smell," without sight. Some scholars think that may lie in the background here. They made mockery of Jesus' claim to Messiahship by blindfolding him, beating him with the fist, and then asking him to identify the one who struck him. Also the attendants "rained blows on him." They slapped him; they caught him with blows. It's a difficult sentence to translate. In one of his predictions of his coming passion, Jesus had foreseen this kind of torture and humiliation. "They will mock him, and spit upon him, and flog him, and kill him" (Mk 9:34). This prophecy was now being fulfilled.

But there was another prophecy about to be fulfilled, and that was Peter's denial of his Lord. While Jesus was being mistreated by members of the Sanhedrin and their servants, Peter was sitting at the fire in the courtyard. Whether he could see clearly what was going on, or whether he discovered later how Jesus had been tormented, he could never get this picture out of his mind. When he wrote his first epistle he had this to say: "Because Christ also suffered for you, leaving you an example, that you should follow in his steps. He committed no sin; no guile was found on his lips; when he was reviled he did not revile in return; when he suffered, he did not threaten; but he trusted him who judges justly; he himself bore our sins in his body on the tree, that we might die to sin and live to righteousness. By his wounds you have been healed" (1 Pet 2:21-23).

Bernard of Clairvaux expressed his deep sorrow and his faith in Christ as he thought of his Lord's suffering, in the following lines: "O sacred Head, now wounded, With grief and shame weighed down; Now scornfully surrounded, With thorns, Thine only crown; O sacred Head, what glory, What bliss till now was Thine! Yet, though despised and gory, I joy to call Thee mine."

Chapter 7

Peter's Denial of his Lord Mark 14:66-72

The apostle Peter has a prominent place in Mark's passion narrative. To begin with, we have Peter's expression of unwavering loyalty to his Master. "Even though all become deserters, I will not," he assured Jesus (v. 29). "Even though I must die with you, I will not deny you" (v. 31).

And then we have that rather sorrowful scene in the garden of Gethsemane, in which Jesus takes Peter, James and John somewhat beyond where the rest of the disciples were, in the hope that they would stand by him as he looked squarely into the face of his imminent death on the cross. But they fell asleep, and when Christ returned to them, after yielding to the Father's will, he asked Peter, "Simon, are you asleep? Could you not keep awake one hour?" (v. 37).

Then followed Jesus' arrest, and Peter, who could not accept the fact that his Lord should be put to death, reacted spontaneously and drew his sword with which he cut off the ear of the high priest's servant. Although Mark does not mention Peter by name in verses 47 and 48, John in his Gospel tells us that it was Peter. Jesus then rebuked him for this act of violence and healed the servant's ear.

After Jesus was arrested and was being taken to the high priest, we read in verse 54, that Peter followed at a distance, right into the court of the high priest. The other disciples had all fled, with the exception of John, who was known to the high priest. Peter then sat down in the courtyard with the guards and warmed himself at the fire they had made.

And that leads us up to the passage that lies before us today, in which we have the tragic story of Peter's denial of his Lord. While the trial of Jesus was going on in the high priest's house, a drama of a different kind was being enacted in the courtyard. Peter's loyalty to Jesus was about to be tested. And although he failed miserably in the end, we have to admire his courage, for to sit down with the servants beside the fire in the courtyard was risky business, and that all the more, because it was Peter who had wounded the servant of the high priest.

I. THE FIRST CHALLENGE TO PETER'S LOYALTY TO JESUS, AND PETER'S RESPONSE

"While Peter was below in the courtyard, one of the servant-girls of the high priest came by. When she saw Peter warming himself she stared at him and said, 'You also were with Jesus, the man from Nazareth.' But he denied it saying, 'I do not know or understand what you are talking about'. And he went out of the fore-court" (v. 66-68).

The word "below" suggests that the high priest's house in which Jesus was being tried, had more than one story. Peter was sitting with the high priest's servants (v. 54). The word "servants" (*huperetes* - literally "under-rower") can also mean attendants, guards, helpers. They could have been temple police who maintained order in the temple precincts. They could have been servants at the disposal of the Sanhedrin for policing purposes. We can't identify these attendants too precisely, but certainly they were not friends of Jesus. The application has often been made, that it is dangerous for followers of Jesus to fraternize with the enemies of Jesus, for that can easily lead to a denial of Jesus. Peter had ventured into the very heart of the enemy citadel. Perhaps he was already sorry for his poor performance in the garden, and was compensating for his failure by putting on a show of bravado.

Be that as it may, one of the servant-women of the high priest came by. John in his Gospel gives us the added information that this woman was the one who guarded the gate to the courtyard. To begin with, she wouldn't let Peter in, but then the disciple who knew the high priest (we assume it was John) went and spoke to her and she opened the gate for Peter (Jo 18:16). And this woman now mounts the first challenge to Peter's loyalty to Jesus.

"When she saw Peter warming himself she stared at him and said, 'You also were with Jesus, the man from Nazareth'" (v. 67). She made no threats; she simply looked intently at Peter and said, you too were with Jesus of Nazareth. It was about as mild a challenge as could have been made, and perhaps the very weakness of the woman was Peter's undoing. Had the servants wanted to seize him and arrest him, he may have put up a fight, but a chance remark by a maid didn't call for a strong stand. It often happens in the Christian life, that we are prepared to face strong opposition to our faith, but then we turn around and fail in little things.

Her reference to Jesus was contemptuous. The text literally reads, "You also were with this Nazarene, this Jesus." To be "with Jesus" meant that he was his disciple. How did she know this? Had she seen Peter in the company with Jesus some time during the days when he taught in the temple? It is next to impossible to think of her as part of the party that arrested Jesus in the company of his disciples in the garden. Many Galileans came to Jerusalem for Passover and they could be recognized by their accent. Had Peter been alone, he might have passed off the woman's remark without comment, but she said it in the hearing of the attendants sitting around the fire, and that put him in an awkward position. And so we have Peter's response to the first challenge of his loyalty to Jesus.

"But he denied it saying, 'I do not know or understand what you are talking about'. And he went out of the fore-court" (v. 68). Peter denied his association with Jesus. Later in the Christian church the word "deny" came to have an even more serious meaning; it meant to apostatize. He shrugs off the woman's comment by suggesting that it was too ridiculous to respond to. "I don't know or understand what you are talking about." He was concerned about his own safety, and by his response tried to get the approval of the bystanders. And so Peter lied about his association with Jesus. A lie often calls forth more lies to cover up what has been said, and that is seen in the denials that now follow.

Peter must have felt uncomfortable with the woman's challenge and his offhand response, and withdraws into the fore-court, the entryway. A number of manuscripts and ancient versions have a little addition here, not found in most English Bibles, although some have it in the footnote as a possible variant. The addition reads: "And the rooster crowed." Some scholars are of the opinion that a copyist added this in the text of Mark because in verse 72 it is said that the rooster crowed a second time. If he crowed a second time, there must have been a first time, and so this comment on the crowing of the rooster was slipped in at this point. But perhaps Mark wanted to mention only the second cock-crow, because Jesus had said that Peter would deny him thrice before the cock crowed twice.

And with that we come to the second challenge to Peter's loyalty to Jesus and to his response.

II. THE SECOND CHALLENGE AND PETER'S RESPONSE

"And the servant-girl, on seeing him, began again to say to the bystanders, 'This man is one of them'. But again he denied it" (vv. 69,70a).

Shifting his position from one part of the courtyard to another did not save Peter from further attacks. He wanted to avoid further confrontations, but he was not yet willing to leave altogether. Perhaps he recalled what he had said earlier, namely, that he would not leave Jesus even if others did.

The woman portress now involves the bystanders. It appears as if the same woman sees Peter at the entrance of the courtyard and speaks to the bystanders: "This man is one of them." The woman knew that Jesus had been the leader of a band of disciples. But Peter denied that he had been a follower of Jesus. The verb "deny" is in the imperfect tense in Greek, which could be read to mean that he denied repeatedly. Peter had been the first of the Twelve who was called by Jesus (Mk 1:16) to be with him (Mk 3:14). And now he denies all that.

And that leads us to the third denial. In the Scriptures, if something is done three times, the implication is, that it is complete, final. "A threefold cord is not quickly broken," declared the Preacher (Eccles. 4:12). "So faith, hope and love abide, these three," writes Paul (1 Cor 13:13). The apostle John speaks of three witnesses: "the Spirit, the water and the blood, and these three agree' (1 Jo 5:8). Scholars have found as many as 60 examples of triplicity in the Synoptic Gospels alone. We shouldn't be surprised, then, when some ministers prefer three-decker sermons. Such sermons are often the target of light banter, but as my colleague, Dr. J. A. Toews, used to say, "A chair with three legs is safer than one with two".

Be that as it may, we have before us the story of a three-fold denial of Jesus by the chief of the apostles, Peter. And we anticipate the day, after the resurrection of our Lord, when Christ will ask Peter three times, "Do you love me?" and restore him to apostleship.

III. THE THIRD CHALLENGE AND PETER'S RESPONSE

"Then after a little while the bystanders again said to Peter, 'Certainly you are one of them, for you are a Galilean.' But he began to curse, and he swore an oath, 'I do not know this man you are taking about'" (vv. 70b,71).

Peter was getting himself progressively into a more difficult situation. When the servant-girl spoke to him the first time, he shrugged it off; suggesting that she was speaking nonsense. But this woman, like all women, didn't want to be treated like an idiot, and as Peter got up to go into the fore-court, she fixed her gaze on him, and let the attendants know that Peter was a member of the Jesus movement. With that she recedes into the background, for now the attendants have caught on.

"Certainly," they said, "You are one of them, for you are a Galilean." Matthew explains how they recognized that he was a Galilean: "Your speech betrays you." Hebrew and Aramaic have a lot of guttural sounds, and it was commonly said, that Galileans couldn't distinguish them very well. For example, they couldn't distinguish between lamb, wool, wine, and donkey. (All words with similar sounds in Aramaic). Peter's pronunciation stuck out among a group of Judeans in the courtyard, and so they concluded that he was a follower of the heretic, Jesus of Nazareth, the Galilean.

That confident challenge, "Certainly you were one of them," called forth a violent protest on the part of Peter. He began to curse. It means to call down a curse on himself, if he was lying, and also to call down a curse on the bystanders, if what they were claiming was true. If we were to use modern language, Peter was saying, "May I be damned, if what I am saying is not the truth."

Because the verb "to curse" is used here without an object, some scholars have suggested, that he cursed Jesus, but that does not seem to be the meaning here. However, later, when Christians were persecuted, their enemies often tried to get them to curse Jesus. After Paul became a Christian, he confessed (Acts 26:11), that in his unbelieving state he had tried to force Christians to blaspheme Jesus. He wasn't successful, for Christians chose rather to die than to curse their Lord. At the beginning of the 2nd century, Pliny, the governor of Bithynia, writes to Trajan, the emperor, and asks for advice on how to treat the Christians. One thing they will not do, he writes: they will not curse Jesus. Paul writes in 1 Corinthians 12:3, "Therefore I want you to understand that no one speaking by the Spirit of God ever says, 'let Jesus be cursed'." However, when Peter denied his Lord, he was more likely calling down a curse on himself and on the bystanders, if they insisted that he belonged to the followers of Jesus.

Not only did he begin to curse, but he bound himself with an oath. His oath was, of course in clear violation of Jesus' teaching in the Sermon on the Mount, "swear not at all" (Mt 5:34). I don't know "this man" you are talking about, he said. Notice that he never once mentions the name of Jesus. He puts as much distance between himself and his Lord as possible. He had completely forgotten what Jesus had said earlier, "Those who are ashamed of me and of my words... of them the Son of Man will be ashamed when he comes in the glory of his Father with the holy angels" (Mk 8:38). Peter had gone as far as he could in denying his Master, and put himself in mortal danger.

Thank God, that's not the end of the story. After he had totally denied his Lord, he heard a rooster crow.

IV. THE COCK-CROW AND PETER'S REPENTANCE

"At that moment the cock crowed for the second time. Then Peter remembered that Jesus had said to him, 'Before the cock crows twice, you will deny me three times.' And he broke down and wept" (v. 72).

Luke adds an interesting detail at this point in the narrative. He says, "The Lord turned and looked at Peter" (22:61). And then Peter remembered what Jesus had said, "Before the cock crows twice, you will deny me three times." It is now early morning. In the Greco-Roman world the dawn or the rising of the sun is associated with the second cock-crow. There is another way of reading this verse. The third watch of the night, i.e., from midnight to 3 AM, was called the "cock-crow." A signal was given with a trumpet when the cock-crow watch ended.

But it is unlikely that the Gospel writers had that in mind; it seems rather more likely that they were in fact speaking of the crowing of a rooster. It sounds a bit bizarre, but 20th century scholars have actually spent nights in Jerusalem to check out the cock-crows.

When Mark says that the cock crowed for the second time, the implication is, that it had crowed once before, but that Peter had paid no attention to it. At least it didn't awaken any memories in him. But when it crowed a second time, he remembered what Jesus had predicted: "Truly I tell you, this day, this very night, before the cock crows twice, you will deny me three times" (v. 30). To that prediction Peter had responded vehemently, "Even though I must die with you, I will not deny you." But he had, and the memory of those words hit him squarely between the eyes, as we say, and it broke him up completely.

"And he broke down and wept." That Peter wept bitterly can be seen from the verb to break down. The imperfect tense of "weep" can be rendered as "he began to weep." But the verb "to break down" (*epibalo*) is hard to translate. Literally it means "to throw upon," and translators have many options:

(a) Having thrown himself to the ground, he began to weep;

(b) Having rushed out, he began to weep;

(c) Having thrown his mind to it, i.e., having remembered what Jesus said, he burst into tears;

(d) Having cast his eyes on Jesus (who had looked at him), he began to cry;

(e) Having thrown clothing over his head, i.e., covering his head in shame, he burst out in tears;

(f) Having beat on himself, i.e., beat his breast, he began to cry.

However we may translate the first verb, the second is plain: Peter burst into tears of remorse and shame. He had done what he had promised never to do. Jesus had told him and others to watch and pray lest they fall into temptation. But Peter, with bravado, had followed Christ in his own strength, and had fallen into temptation. Now he lies on the ground defeated, one might say.

V. CONCLUSION

The Gospel of Mark was written to the Christian community in Rome, and this story of Peter's denial was a warning to the readers of Mark's Gospel to stand firm and be faithful when put to the test. Toward the end of the century John wrote the book of Revelation in which he commends the church at Pergamum: "I know where you are living, where Satan's throne is. Yet you are holding fast to my name, and you did not deny your faith in me even in the days of Antipas my witness, my faithful one, who was killed among you, where Satan lives" (Rev 2:13).

The day would come when Peter, who repented deeply and was later restored to apostleship, would pay the ultimate price for his loyalty to Jesus, for according to tradition he was crucified in Rome. However, since he felt it was too great an honor for him to be put to death like his Lord, he asked his tormentors to crucify him upside down. Never again would he be ashamed of Christ.

The story of Peter's denial has always had a two-fold message for Christian readers. On the one hand, it has always been read as a warning not to be presumptuous, but to recognize one's weaknesses. It reminds us to pray as Jesus taught us to pray in the Lord's Prayer, "Lead us not into temptation, but deliver us from evil." We dare not sit in judgment over Peter and think that we are immune from such failures as are recorded in this story. Also, we should learn from this account, that failure in a small thing, often leads to greater failures. From his response to what appeared to Peter as an idle remark by a servant-girl, he sank deeper and deeper into sin, until he utterly denied any connection with Jesus.

However, the story was told also, no doubt, to give hope to those who had fallen into sin; who had failed. This narrative would never have been written if Peter had not repented and had not been restored to fellowship with Jesus by his grace. And so we have a story that not only warns us of the danger of trusting in our own strength, but also one that holds out hope to those who are keenly aware of their failures.

This man, who had denied Christ so shamefully, gave the rest of his life to faithful and fruitful service in the kingdom of God. Failure is never the last word in our Christian experience. There is hope even for the blackest sinner. Christ Jesus is able "to save to the uttermost those who come to God by him" (Heb 7:25). Just as Christ brought Peter back from the depths of shame to the place of leadership among the apostles, so he can raise us up from the darkness of failure into the sunlight of his wonderful grace.

Chapter 8

Jesus before the Governor Mark 15:1-15

In the passage before us, Pontius Pilate plays an important role, and that calls for a brief description of the political situation in Palestine at the time of Christ's death.

When Jesus was born, Herod the Great was king over all Palestine, by the grace of the Romans. It was he who carried out the massacre of the children of Judea. He died in 4 B.C., according to our modern way of reckoning. The Romans then divided the land among three of his sons: Antipas got Galilee and Perea; Philip received the northern territories; and Archelaus was given Samaria, Judea and Idumea in the south.

Archelaus became known for his cruelty and so when the holy family returned from Egypt, after escaping the wrath of Herod the Great, and when they heard that Archelaus was made ruler over Judea, they settled in Nazareth of Galilee (Mt 2:22).

Archelaus ruled over southern Palestine for 10 years (4 B.C. to A.D. 6) and was then deposed by the Romans for his misrule. The Romans then brought in a governor, sometimes called procurator, who had his seat, not in Jerusalem, but in the coastal city of Caesarea Maritima.

Judea was a troublesome province, and by the time Jesus was brought before the governor, Pilate, several other governors had already come and gone. Pilate must have been a man of some ability, for he ruled for ten years. Usually the Roman governors didn't last longer than about four years.

Pilate had assumed his governorship in A.D. 26, and although he had his residence in Caesarea on the coast, he regularly came to Jerusalem for the festivals, when feelings of Jewish nationalism tended to flare up. The Romans allowed the Sanhedrin in Jerusalem to govern the every day life of the Jews, although the Romans reserved the right to appoint the high priest.

Capital punishment lay in the hands of the Roman governor, and so after the Sanhedrin had condemned Jesus to death, they wanted the governor to pronounce the verdict. Consequently the trial of Jesus now moves away from the Sanhedrin to the governor's residence.

The Sanhedrin had found Jesus guilty of blasphemy. However, the Jewish authorities knew that such a charge would not be taken seriously by Pilate. They would have to come up with a political charge, if they were to get anywhere with the procurator. And so they decided to charge Jesus with claiming to be king, as can be seen from verse 2. That charge could easily be based on Jesus' claim to Messiahship, for in the eyes of the Jews Messiah was to be a king who would sit on the throne of David and restore Israel to former greatness.

I. THE ARRAIGNMENT BEFORE PILATE

A. The Decision of the Sanhedrin (v. 1). "As soon as it was morning, the chief priests held a consultation with the elders and scribes and the whole court. They bound Jesus, led him away, and handed him over to Pilate."

There has been some debate over which residence Pilate and his soldiers occupied when they came to the festival. One suggestion is the Antonia Fortress, a castle refurbished by Herod the Great and named after Mark Anthony. It dominated the NW corner of the Temple area and gave the soldiers easy access to the temple.

However, Herod the Great had also built a palace in

Jerusalem for himself, and some scholars believe that Pilate and his troops would have taken up residence in Herod's palace. Such details are of interest, but they do not affect the message of the Passion narrative.

The opening verse of chapter 15 is actually transitional. The Sanhedrin had examined Jesus and decided that he deserved to die. Now they have a consultation among themselves, to decide on their next move. The mention of chief priests, elders and scribes, makes it clear that this is a reference to the Sanhedrin. Chief priests would include Caiaphas, former high priests, and members of families from which the high priests came. The elders represented the Jewish aristocracy, important families. The scribes were the legal experts. At this time the Sanhedrin was dominated by Sadducees, although Pharisees were also represented, particularly among the scribes. Whether all 71 members were present or not, is another matter. But evidently they had a quorum.

It may appear from verse 1 as if these three groups met separately, but the expression "the whole Sanhedrin" makes it clear that they were simply representatives within this larger governing body. After the names of the three groups, we might add, "in short, the whole Sanhedrin."

This Jewish council knew that the governor held court early in the morning, and so they had to hurry to get their act together before daybreak.

But now they were ready, and so they bound Jesus, i.e., handcuffed him, and led him away from the high priest's palace to Pilate's temporary residence. Here they gave him over to the governor.

By using the expression "handed him over," Mark may well have had Isaiah 53:6 in mind, where it is said of the Suffering Servant: "The Lord gave him over for our sins" (LXX). Moreover, Jesus himself had predicted that the Son of Man would be handed over to the chief priests and the scribes and that they would condemn him to death. And, also, that they would hand him over to the Gentiles (Mk 10:33). And that's what happened here.

    B. The Question of Pilate (v. 2-4). "Pilate asked him, 'Are you the king of the Jews?' He answered him, 'You say so.' Then the chief priests accused him of many things. Pilate asked him again, 'Have you no answer? See how many charges they bring against you'".

Since Palestinian Jews at that time were generally bilingual, it is assumed that Pilate spoke Greek when he questioned Jesus. Had he spoken in Latin, which was the language of the judiciary in the Empire generally, the translator might have been mentioned. Aramaic was the common everyday language of Palestinian Jews, but it is very unlikely that Pilate was conversant in Aramaic. Again, it's an interesting question, but it does not affect the Passion narrative.

    To the question which Pilate asked Jesus, "Are you the King of the Jews?" Jesus gave an ambiguous answer. He didn't say, "I am," even though he knew that as Messiah he was the King of Israel. But he also knew that Pilate had a different understanding of kingship. For Jesus to claim outright that he was the King of the Jews would have meant, for Pilate, that he was an insurrectionist and that he was guilty of treason, which would have called for the death penalty. Actually Pilate asked the question in a rather insulting manner: "You there, are you the king of the Jews?" And so Jesus answered: "You said it." He didn't deny that he was Israel's King, but he did not want Pilate to think that he was a political revolutionary who was out to lead a crusade against the Romans.

    From verse 3 we learn, however, that the high priests accused him of many things. Mark doesn't say what they were, but if we turn to Luke 23:2 we have the following accusations: "We found this man perverting our nation, forbidding us to pay taxes to the emperor, and saying that he himself is the Messiah, a king." For these accusers it was clear, that for someone to claim to be Messiah meant also that he thought of himself as king.

During Jesus' lifetime several Messiahs had already arisen and had attracted followers. These revolutionary movements were always put down with great cruelty by the Romans. The Sanhedrin obviously wanted to portray Jesus as one of these Messiahs who threatened the Roman rule.

Jesus' answer to Pilate's question is very instructive. "You said it'" meant a half Yes and a half No. It's your statement not mine. I think of kingship in different categories than you do. In the Gospel of John we have some added words that Jesus spoke to Pilate which are not recorded in the Synoptics. He tells Pilate, Yes, I am a king, but my kingdom is not of this world. If it were, then my followers would fight (Jo 18:36). The Jews wanted Pilate to think of Jesus as a rival king, an agitator for Israel's political independence. But Jesus divorces himself completely from all insurrectionist movements of his day. He will establish a different kind of kingdom and he will do so by suffering and dying for the sins of the world.

Perhaps we should recall the story of the Magi who came to Jerusalem, asking where the new-born king of the Jews could be found. King Herod was outraged, for every threat to Roman rule was brutally suppressed. Matthew, who tells the story, adds that all of Jerusalem was afraid, for they didn't know how Herod would respond to the news that a rival king had appeared.

Pilate presses Jesus to respond to the other charges that the Jewish leaders were bringing against him, but they were all false charges, and Jesus did not reply to them.

C. The Silence of Jesus (v. 5). "But Jesus made no further reply, so that Pilate was amazed."

Jesus had said nothing to the false charges brought before the Sanhedrin (14:60), and again he was silent in the face of the calumnies heaped on him before Pilate. Pilate was surprised that Jesus would not respond to the many charges laid against him.

Jesus could easily have unmasked his adversaries, as he had so often done when they attacked him verbally during his ministry. But now he is silent. It was a tragic silence, coming from the recognition that speech was quite useless in this situation.

At the same time it was a sublime silence, like a sheep before its shearers is dumb, to use the words of Isaiah 53:7. This silence of Jesus made a deep impression on Pilate, this hardened man of the world. Normally an accused person would do everything within his power to repudiate such false charges. Jesus' silence impressed Pilate so profoundly, that he "marvelled."

The apostle Peter later wrote in his first epistle, "When he was abused, he did not return abuse; when he suffered, he did not threaten; but he entrusted himself to the one who judges justly" (2:23).

According to Luke's account, Pilate was convinced of Jesus' innocence. He says to the chief priests and the crowd: "I find no basis for an accusation against this man" (Lk 23:4). However, since the enemies of Jesus continue to hurl charges against him, Pilate looks for a way out of his dilemma, and suggests a Passover amnesty.

II. JESUS OR BARABBAS

A. The Custom (v. 6). "Now at the festival he used to release a prisoner for them, anyone for whom they asked."

Mark omits the trial of Jesus before Herod Antipas of Galilee, who had come down to Jerusalem for the festival — not because he was so religious, but because it was politically advantageous for him to show respect for Jewish customs. And when Pilate discovered that Jesus came from Galilee, he hoped to get him off his hands by sending him over to Herod, who ruled over Galilee. Herod felt flattered that the Roman governor would pay him such respect. Herod questioned Jesus and hoped he would perform a miracle, but Jesus again remained completely silent. After his soldiers had mocked Jesus, Herod sent him back to Pilate. From that day on Herod and Pilate were friends. But Mark skips this episode.

We are back now at Pilate's temporary residence. Pilate was convinced that Jesus was innocent and would have set him free, had he not feared the violent reaction to such a decision by the Jewish authorities.

The Jewish authorities had already forced Pilate to back down on several other occasions prior to this event. Shortly after he became governor, he sent troops, carrying Roman standards, to Jerusalem. The images on these standards always offended the Jews, and so he sent the soldiers in at night. When the Jews discovered what had happened, they came to Caesarea en masse and demanded that they be removed. Pilate responded by threatening to kill the protesters. But when he saw that they were willing to die for their cause, he backed down. So they knew from past experience, that if they pressed the governor hard enough, they would get their way.

Pilate's effort to avoid passing judgment on Jesus by sending him off to Herod had failed. Now he will try another approach: the paschal amnesty. Mark mentions that it was Pilate's custom to release a prisoner at the request of the Jews to show them a special favor at Passover. Amnesty implied that the prisoner was guilty, and Pilate thought it would please the Jews if he agreed with them that Jesus was guilty, even though he himself believed he was innocent. Roman justice went begging at this point. Pilate did not have the backbone to stand up for what was right. He knew Jesus was innocent but he also knew that he couldn't set Jesus free without causing a riot. His hope now was that the Jerusalem crowds would choose Jesus. But his plan misfired. The Jewish leaders had a consultation and decided rather to choose Barabbas, a murderer, a revolutionary, as candidate for the paschal amnesty. Matthew informs us that they then went ahead and persuaded the crowds to agree with them (27:20).

B. The Murderer (v. 7). "Now a man called Barabbas was in prison with the rebels who had committed murder during the insurrection."

Barabbas has an interesting name. Some think it was his patronymic, and not his first name. ***Bar*** in Aramaic is the word for "son," and ***abba*** is the word for "father." Literally then the meaning would be "son of a father." There is however another possibility, namely, "son of a rabbi."

What is interesting is that Matthew, according to some manuscripts gives him the name "Jesus," i.e., Jesus bar abbas. And, according to Matthew 27:17, Pilate asks, "Whom shall I release, Jesus Barabbas or Jesus the Christ?" Although not many manuscripts have the word "Jesus" before Barabbas, it may be that a later copyist dropped it deliberately because he did not want this prisoner to have the same name as Jesus the Christ. Some English Bibles (such as NEB and TNIV) have it; other's don't. And so there is some uncertainly about his full name.

Barabbas must have taken part in a local insurrection against the Romans, for Luke says it happened in Jerusalem (Lk 23:19). In this insurrection the rebels, including Barabbas, had committed murder. It is hard for us to understand that the Jerusalem crowd would ask Pilate to let this murderer go free, and crucify Jesus. However, Jews at that time usually looked with favor upon all freedom fighters who protested against the Roman yoke, much to the annoyance of the Romans.

C. The Offer (vv. 8-11). "So the crowd came and began to ask Pilate to do for them according to his custom. Then he answered them, 'Do you want me to release for you the King of the Jews?' For he realized that it was out of jealousy the chief priests had handed him over. But the chief priests stirred up the crowd to have him release Barabbas for them instead."

So far Mark has mentioned only the Jewish hierarchy as opponents of Jesus, but now the crowd gets involved. They come up, perhaps from down town. There is, however, no reason to believe that this was the same crowd that had earlier shouted "Hosanna" when Jesus rode into Jerusalem, although some of those who earlier acclaimed Jesus as the son of David may have turned against Jesus, when they saw that he was beaten, bleeding, and bound.

The Jewish leaders "stirred up" the crowd to ask for Barabbas. Just how they went about persuading the crowd to choose Barabbas instead of Jesus, is not stated, but the story illustrates how people can be influenced for evil. And today with all the mass media to which the public is exposed, even Christians can be led astray. Living in a secular world, with secular values held before us constantly, it is little wonder that believers are influenced by this-worldly points of view.

To Pilate's great disappointment, they ask him to release Barabbas—the last person a Roman governor would want to see go free, because he was a revolutionary and a threat to the Roman power. Pilate now found himself in a terrible bind, especially since he knew full well that it was out of jealousy that the Jews wanted Jesus out of the way. The Jewish leaders could not stand the hold that Jesus' message had on the common folk. If Pilate had secretly hoped that the crowd would choose Jesus as his candidate for the Passover amnesty, he was badly mistaken. They had forced his hand. And so Jesus will die while the murderer will go free. And that's the gospel in a nutshell. Jesus dies in the place of sinners. He dies a substitutionary death.

III. JESUS CONDEMNED TO DIE

A. The Outcry (vv. 12,13). "Pilate spoke to them again, 'Then what do you wish me to do with the man you call the King of the Jews?' They shouted back, 'Crucify him'!"

Pilate is not yet willing to concede defeat and throws out the question to the crowd: What shall I do with Jesus? Did he hope they would change their minds about their choice and ask for Jesus' release as well? Pilate's question sounds a bit sarcastic: What then shall I do with this man whom you call King of the Jews? That was certainly not the kind of title they would wish to ascribe to Jesus. It must have stung the Jewish leaders and offended them terribly.

According to John's Gospel they answer: "We have no other king but Caesar." In fact they threaten Pilate: "If you release this man, you are no longer Caesar's friend" (Jo 19:12). Very likely Pilate feared that they would accuse him before the emperor and, in fact, that's what eventually happened. As a result, Pilate was removed from his post.

There is then something insulting in the way Pilate asks the question, as to what to do with Jesus. But there is also something rather ironical about it. A Roman governor, who had the authority to carry out capital punishment, asks the crowd what he should do with Jesus. And the crowd tells him. Jews tell a Roman judge what to do with a rival king.

They know, of course, what to do with a rival king: he must be crucified. In Mark's Gospel we have three predictions by Jesus of his impending death (8:31; 9:31; 10:34). In all of them Jesus says that he will be killed, not that he will be crucified. Here for the first time in Mark it is made clear, how Jesus will be killed: by crucifixion. That was the most barbaric method of putting criminals to death.

B. The Verdict (vv. 14,15). "Pilate asked them, 'Why, what evil has he done?' But they shouted all the more, 'Crucify him!' So Pilate, wishing to satisfy the crowd, released Barabbas for them; and after flogging Jesus, he handed him over to be crucified."

Once again Pilate tried to spare Jesus by underscoring his innocence, but the fierce outcry of the crowd brought all these efforts to an end. The second outcry is even greater than the first. They shouted even more, even louder.

According to Matthew 27:24, Pilate by now saw that he

could do nothing, and that a riot was about to break out. And so he took water and washed his hands before the crowd, saying "I am innocent of this man's blood." Washing hands was an ancient gesture to underscore a person's innocence (cf. Deut 21:6f.). The Psalmist says, "I wash my hands in innocence" (73:13). That idiom has come into the English language and even people who don't know the Bible speak of washing their hands of some evil deed. In the apocryphal Gospel of Peter there is this added comment: "But of the Jews no one washed his hands." In other words, they assumed responsibility for the death of Jesus. "His blood be upon us and on our children," they cry (Mt 27:25). That word has unfortunately been abused in history, to blame the Jewish people as a whole for all generations of being Christ-killers. This has led to senseless persecution and pogroms and the endless shedding of blood.

However, Pilate cannot escape his guilt simply by a symbolical act of washing his hands. He had the authority to set Jesus free, but he knuckled under. What we have here is a travesty of Roman justice. To condemn an innocent person to death, was contrary to all Roman and Jewish jurisprudence. And so in the end Pilate turns out to be a rather pathetic figure. He releases Barabbas, the bandit, the murderer, the freedom-fighter, and hands over Jesus to be crucified.

Once again we have the expression "handed over." In his predictions of his death Jesus had said repeatedly that he would be handed over. When Judas arrived with the arresting crowd, Jesus said, the Son of Man is being handed over. The Sanhedrin decided to hand him over to Pilate (15:1). In verse 10 of our text we are told, that they handed him over because of jealousy. And now Pilate hands him over to be crucified. Although these actions by various individuals, of handing Jesus over underscore the evil that was perpetrated against the Son of Man, behind the scenes God is handing over his Son, for the salvation of the world. Peter, in his Pentecost address, says, "This man, handed over to you according to the definite plan and foreknowledge of God, you crucified and killed, by the hands of those outside the law" (Acts 2:23).

Before Jesus is taken away to be crucified, Pilate decides to have Jesus scourged. Perhaps he hoped that this cruel punishment would satisfy the crowd and convince them that Jesus had been punished enough; in this way, saving him from crucifixion. In fact in John's Gospel we are told that Pilate led the bruised and beaten Jesus into the open for all to see and said, "Behold, the man." But the crowd had made up its mind and there was no return.

The flogging of Jesus is reported in one line only, both in Matthew and in Mark. Luke, in fact, omits the reference to the flogging altogether. It almost appears as if the Gospel writers were hesitant to report it. The readers would have known what scourging involved. Victims often collapsed and died under this torture. The victim was stripped naked, tied to a post or pillar, and beaten as long as the strength of the tormentors lasted. In contrast to Jewish law, where 40 lashes were the maximum, there was no maximum in the case of the Romans.

Moreover, the Roman lash (*flagella* in Latin) often had leather thongs studded with sharp pieces of metal or bone, and it literally tore the person's back to ribbons. No Roman citizen was to be treated this way. When Paul was later caught in the temple, the Roman tribune was about to tie Paul up in preparation for flogging, until Paul invoked his Roman citizenship, and then he left off.

When Josephus, the Jewish historian, was governor of Galilee in the sixties, he had some of his opponents scourged (he writes) until their entrails hung out. The flogging evidently was in preparation for crucifixion. The normal way of carrying out the death penalty in ancient Israel was by stoning. Luke in Acts 7 gives us an account of how Stephen, the first Christian martyr, was stoned to death. The Romans normally carried out capital punishment by beheading with the sword. We have an example of that in Acts 12:1, where the apostle James, one of the Zebedee brothers, was beheaded. But Jesus was to receive the worst form of punishment: crucifixion. And so the cross for all times has become the symbol of the Christian faith.

The late Malcolm Muggeridge of literary fame grew up in a home in which the cross was derided. And yet as a boy he felt attracted to the story of Christ's death. Often he would read the story under the covers, as he lay in bed, using a flashlight, so that his parents wouldn't find out that he was reading the NT. Late in life, when he had finally become a believer, he felt deeply grieved that he had rejected the cross and what it stood for in his youth. He writes: "I should have worn it over my heart; carried it, a precious standard, never to be wrested out of my hands; even though I fell, still borne it aloft. It should have been my cult, my uniform, my language, my life. I shall have no excuse; I can't say I didn't know. I knew from the beginning, and turned away."

Those of us, who by God's grace have embraced the cross and its saving message, can join the hymn-writer and confess, "In the cross of Christ I glory, Tow'ring o'er the wrecks of time; All the light of sacred story, Gathers round its head sublime."

Chapter 9

They Crucified Him Mark 15:16-26

At the heart of the Christian gospel stands the cross of Christ. Other religions also have symbols by which they are identified, but Christianity has the cross. The lotus flower has become associated with Buddhism. Modern Judaism has adopted the so-called Star of David, a hexagram formed by combining two triangles. Islam, like Judaism, another monotheistic religion, is symbolized by the crescent. But the Christian gospel is called "the word of the cross" (1 Cor 1:18).

Although the cross may not have been the first symbol of the Christian movement, for the symbol of the fish is quite early, the cross eventually became its universal symbol. Early Christians could have chosen other symbols, such as the manger, the carpenter's bench, the apron Jesus wore when he washed the disciples' feet. But, as early as the second century, believers drew and painted the cross, and even made the sign of the cross as an expression of their faith.

This is really remarkable when one remembers the horror with which crucifixion was regarded in the ancient world. The enemies of Christianity lost no opportunity to ridicule the Christian claim, that the one who died on the cross, by order of the governor, Pontius Pilate, was the savior of the world. But in the wisdom of God the death of the sinless Son of God, procured salvation for the entire sinful human race.

Today we want to follow our Lord to the cross. Our passage begins with the mockery and abuse of Jesus before he is led away to be crucified. The crucifixion itself is passed over almost in silence. "And they crucified him" (v. 24). No details of this wretched method of putting people to death are given. However, the Evangelists tell us about some of the attendant circumstances of the crucifixion of Jesus.

Before Jesus is led away to Calvary, he is abused and mocked by Pilate's soldiers, and that's where we want to begin our study today.

I. THE MOCKERY AND ABUSE OF JESUS

The soldiers took Jesus and led him inside the governor's headquarters, the courtyard of the palace. This is the first explicit reference to soldiers. Jesus had been taken captive by a crowd sent by the Sanhedrin armed with swords and clubs. All night long he had been in the hands of the Jewish authorities. Early Friday morning they brought him before Pilate, who passed the death sentence. And now he is in the hands of Pilate's soldiers. These soldiers were not necessarily Italians, but provincials, recruited in Palestine from among the non-Jewish population—Samaritans, Syrians, and others. They were generally a cruel lot, but all of them were fiercely loyal to Caesar and deeply anti-Jewish. They now lead Jesus inside the "Praetorium." That's a Latin word which originally designated an army officer's tent, but then it came to be used also for the governor's residence.

The entire cohort of soldiers now gather to make fun of Jesus. A cohort could be anywhere from 200 to 600 men, but there is no reason to believe that all the soldiers participated in the mockery. They now clothe Jesus in a purple cloak.

A. The Royal Garment (vv. 16,17). "Then the soldiers led him into the courtyard of the palace (the governor's headquarters); and they called together the whole cohort. And they clothed him in a purple cloak."

We have already had one account of how Jesus was mocked, when he was accused of blasphemy (14:65). That was in the palace of the high priest. Luke also reports the mockery which Jesus had to endure when Pilate sent him over to Herod Antipas, who happened to be in Jerusalem for the feast. That was an attempt by Pilate to get him off his hands. And now we have another mockery scene in Pilate's residence.

Matthew explains (27:28) that they first took off his clothes, before they put the purple cloak on him. No doubt it was something they had at hand, and very likely it was a soldier's scarlet garment, meant to symbolize royalty. Some of them must have been present when Pilate questioned Jesus in the presence of the Jewish crowd about his claim to kingship, and so they dress Jesus up crudely as a king.

B. The Crown of Thorns (v. 17b). "And after twisting some thorns into a crown, they put it on him."

The Gospel writers say nothing about the pain caused by such a crown; it is mentioned only as part of the mockery. This word "crown" (Greek: ***stephanos***) means a wreath, not a *diadema* (a purple headband). This was a wreath made of thorns, imitating the laurel wreath worn at times by emperors.

What kind of thorns they used is not stated; thorn bushes could be found all over Palestine. Some think it may even have been made of palm spines. The picture of Jesus wearing a crown of thorns in mockery, has made a deep impression on Christians all through the centuries. One can see this particularly in our hymnody. In the twelfth century, Bernard of Clairvaux wrote: "O sacred head now wounded, With grief and shame weighed down. Now scornfully surrounded, With thorns, Thine only crown. O sacred Head what glory, What bliss till now was thine. I marvel at the story, I joy to call thee mine."

C. The Salutation and Abuse (vv. 18,19). "And they began saluting him, 'The King of the Jews!' They struck his head with a reed, spat upon him, and knelt down in homage to him."

The word salute is not a military salute; the word ordinarily means "to greet." Here it is used in the sense of acclamation. The emperor in those days was greeted with *Ave Caesar* (Hail, Caesar). What we have here is a burlesque of the acclamation given to royalty. The address is derogatory: "Hail, King of the Jews." They said it mockingly and had no inkling of the fact, that by his suffering and death he was about to establish his reign over the hearts and lives of millions of people all over the world.

The empire of the Caesars is long gone; it was built up by brute force, with spear and sword. But the kingdom which Jesus founded, lasts forever. It was established by sacrificial suffering and death. He was indeed the Son of David to whom God had promised an eternal throne (2 Sam 7:16), but attains to eternal kingship by assuming the role of the Suffering Servant of Isaiah 53.

The mockery of the King soon turns into physical abuse. Mark uses imperfect tenses for striking and spitting and bending their knees, and that means they kept on doing this; they repeated these actions. Spitting was not only grossly offensive; it was probably also meant to be a parody of the kiss of homage, so customary in the Near East at that time. Bending the knees, or falling on one's knees, was a sign of respect for superiors. It was also a well-known posture in prayer. Here it is a kind of synonym for worship. They fell on their knees and worshipped him. It was of course mock worship, and it anticipated the mockery that Jesus' followers would have to endure in the coming decades.

In Rome, on the Palatine Hill, in the rooms which served as a training school for imperial pages, there was discovered a graffito (c. A.D. 225) with a crucified donkey, and a boy worshiping it. Crude letters underneath read: "Alexamenus worships god." Evidently those preparing for imperial service mocked Christianity, a minor superstition as they thought of it, involving the worship of a crucified Christ.

"After mocking him, they stripped him of the purple cloak, and put his own clothes on him. Then they led him out to crucify him" (v. 20). Normally a condemned criminal was led to the cross naked, being whipped on the way there. But evidently the Romans had made a concession to Jewish sensitivities with respect to public nudity. Jesus had already been scourged, and so there is no reference to another scourging which regularly occurred prior to crucifixion. Whether they took the crown of thorns from his head as they led him off to be crucified is not stated. Earliest Christian art shows Jesus hanging on the cross without his crown of thorns. Later portrayals of Jesus on the cross, however, often picture him still wearing the crown of thorns.

The soldiers then lead Jesus away to be crucified. We are not told how many soldiers were involved, but according to John's Gospel, they divided Jesus' clothes among themselves, when they nailed him to the cross, and also it is stated that they divided them into four (19:23). From that one might infer that four soldiers were given the grim task of carrying out the crucifixion of Jesus.

Crucifixion was considered to be so hideous a manner of putting a person to death, that the Roman Cicero wrote, "Even the mere word 'cross' must remain far, not only from the lips of the citizens of Rome, but also from their thoughts, their eyes, their ears."

Unfortunately Cicero's countrymen did use this method of executing the vilest of criminals, bandits, revolutionaries, and other unruly elements. The chief reason for its use was its efficacy as a deterrent. It was carried out publicly as a warning to other would-be criminals. Crucifixion had come into the empire from the farther East and the Romans took it over, thinking it was an effective way of keeping law and order in the country. But it also satisfied that primitive lust for revenge and cruelty — something not absent in our Western world either. Crucifixion represented the uttermost humiliation. A naked victim displayed publicly in a prominent place, at crossroads or on high ground. With Deuteronomy 21:23 in the background, the Jews in particular would be aware of this aspect of crucifixion, for one who hangs upon the tree is an accursed one of God, it was said. The humiliation of crucifixion was aggravated by the fact that the victims were as a rule not buried, but served as food for wild beasts and birds of prey. But, in the words of the writer to the Hebrews, our Lord "endured the cross, disregarding the shame, and has taken his seat at the right hand of the throne of God" (12:2).

And now we want to make our way to Calvary.

II. THE WAY TO THE CROSS

A. Simon the Cyrenian (v. 21). "They compelled a passerby, who was coming in from the country, to carry his cross; it was Simon of Cyrene, the father of Alexander and Rufus."

Jesus was now led away to the place of crucifixion which, John tells us, was near the city (19:20), "outside the city gate" (Heb 13:12). According to Jewish custom, a blasphemer was to be taken outside the camp and stoned. And once Israel settled in the land, "outside the camp" was understood as "outside the city."

Jesus had been tried before Annas, before the Sanhedrin, before Herod, and before Pilate during the night and early morning. He had been tormented by the Sanhedrin, Herod's servants, and Pilate's soldiers. It is now Friday morning and Jesus is led through the crowded city, carrying the cross-beam to which he will be nailed. How long our Lord carried this cross-beam is not stated, but the Roman soldiers in charge must have feared that Jesus could die before they reached the place of execution. And so they impressed a passerby into service.

The word "impress" is found also in Matthew 5:41, where Jesus said, "If someone forces you to go one mile, go with him two," and that was a reference to what the occupying power, the Romans, often demanded of Jews. A tap on the shoulder with a soldier's spear was all that was required to demand such a service.

As Jesus was led to his death, a North-African happened to come by. He hailed from Cyrene, modern Libya. There were other Jews from Cyrene in Jerusalem; they even had a synagogue there (Acts 6:9). This man happened to be coming from the field or country. Whether he had come from Cyrene to attend Passover or whether he was now a resident of Judea is not stated. All we know is, that he was the father of Alexander and Rufus. Since Mark wrote his Gospel for Christians, he must have assumed that his Roman readers would be interested in these names. Paul greets a certain Rufus in his letter to the Romans, but it is not certain whether that's the same man. Rufus is a Latin name, whereas Alexander is a Greek name. Perhaps they had in the meantime become Christians and were known to the readers of Mark's Gospel.

In 1941 Israeli archaeologists found a burial cave of Cyrenian Jews and an ossuary (a receptacle with the bones of the dead) on the slope of the Kidron Valley. This ossuary had an inscription: "Alexander, son of Simon." It is intriguing to think that this may have been the grave of Simon and his family.

Imagine how Simon must have felt, when he was coerced into this shameful act of carrying the cross-beam for Jesus. Did Jesus speak to him? Did Simon become a believer after he witnessed Christ's death on the cross? Luke says that Simon carried the cross "behind Jesus." That became the language of discipleship: taking up one's cross and following Jesus.

Jesus has now reached the top of the hill called Golgatha.

B. The Place of a Skull (v.22). "Then they brought Jesus to the place called Golgatha, which means the place of a skull."

The word "brought" (*phero*) can also mean to carry, and some scholars suggest that Jesus by now was so weak, that he quite literally had to be carried or helped along. The place of crucifixion is designated by Mark by both its Semitic name, Golgotha, and its Greek name, ***kranios*** meaning skull (our word cranium). In Latin the word skull is ***calva*** and we get Calvary in our English versions, ever since Wycliffe translated the Bible from Latin into English (1382 AD).

The place was probably so named because the hill looked like a skull, a smooth rounded hilltop. There is a Christian legend that claims it was the place where Adam's skull lay buried. That is quite fanciful, but we can understand why Christians would make that connection, since Christ is the last Adam who died to undo the damage done by the first Adam.

However, other scholars think the place was called "skull," because of the skulls that lay around from former executions.

In the 4th century, Constantine had a basilica built at the spot where it was thought that Jesus was crucified, and this "Church of the Holy Sepulchre" stands there to this day. However, there has been much debate about the exact spot where our Lord was put to death, and the Gospel writers are much more interested in the meaning of Christ's death, than the topography of Calvary.

Although the distance between Pilate's residence and Golgotha may not have been very great, the Roman soldiers very likely took a circuitous route through the city, so that as many people as possible might see with their own eyes how Rome treated rivals to its authority, and be duly warned. When they finally arrived at the place of crucifixion, they tried to give Jesus wine mixed with myrrh, but he refused to take it.

C. The Offering of Wine (v.23). "And they offered him wine mixed with myrrh; but he did not take it."

Just who is meant when Mark says "they" offered him wine, is not clear. It may have been the Roman soldiers; others think the women who were witnesses to Jesus' death are meant. In the book of Proverbs it is said, "Give strong drink to him who is ready to perish and wine to those in bitter distress; when they drink they will forget their misery" (31:6). The Babylonian Talmud evidently knows of a group of Jerusalem women who, as an act of piety, gave a vessel of wine to people condemned to death, which contained some frankincense to numb the pain.

Why they put myrrh, that is perfume, into the wine on this occasion, we do not know, except that aromatic wines were greatly prized in antiquity. No doubt it was intended to alleviate the suffering. Why Jesus refused the drink is not stated. Was it because Jesus wanted to drink the cup of suffering which his Father had given him without a painkiller? Or was it because Jesus had said that he would not drink of the fruit of the vine until the kingdom of God would come in all its glory. But that then raises the question, why he accepted the drink later when he hung on the cross (v. 36).

And with that we come to the crucifixion with Mark reports in the briefest manner possible.

III. THE CRUCIFIXION

A. The Account (v. 24a)."And they crucified him." Four words in English, only three in Greek! Not a word is said about the form of the cross or about how Jesus was nailed to it. Nothing is said about the agony, the pain, the blood. We have a lot of information about the practice of crucifixion from outside the NT. The readers of Mark, of course, were familiar with this gruesome method of execution and so the Evangelist refrains from going into the gory details.

The word "cross" gives us the image of two beams crossing each other. But crosses came in different forms: the upright stake, the X-shaped cross and the cross that was T-shaped. Very likely Jesus was forced to lie down with his arms stretched out, while his hands were nailed to the cross-beam. The vertical stake would have been there in readiness for the planned execution. The cross-beam was then hoisted up and affixed to the upright stake. In the case of Jesus they also nailed his feet to the upright stake. In 1968 a team of Israeli soldiers discovered an ossuary in a graveyard NE of Jerusalem with heel bones transfixed with a single nail about five inches long. A piece of wood still clung to the end of the nail. This was concrete evidence for the practice of nailing victims to a cross.

Crosses were usually only high enough to lift the victim above the ground. In the case of Jesus it must have been higher, for later, when they wanted to give him to drink, they had to use a stick with a sponge on it to reach Jesus' mouth. To prevent asphyxiation and to prolong the agony, a body support was sometimes affixed to the upright stake. But our Gospel writers report that Jesus died relatively quickly. In fact the centurion was surprised that he had died so soon.

B. The Division of the Clothes (v. 24b). "And they divided his clothes among them, casting lots to decide what each should take."

The language of this verse comes from Psalm 22:18, a Psalm which Jesus later quoted as he hung on the cross. Mark simply uses these Psalm-words to describe the dividing of Jesus' clothes. The normal Roman practice was to crucify the criminal naked but, we are told, they made a special concession to Jewish sensitivities in this regard and allowed the victim to have at least a loincloth. Whether that was so in Jesus' case, we do not know, but certainly he was stripped of his clothing before he was lifted up to die on the cross.

In the Gospel of John we are given a few details not mentioned in the Synoptics. He tells us that they divided his clothing among four soldiers (19:23), and that they cast lots so see who would get his tunic. According to Mark, they cast lots for the other pieces of clothing. These would include the turban or head covering, the sandals, the sash or belt, and an undergarment. It is the outer garment that is singled out in John's Gospel, for they would have had to tear it in four pieces if they each wanted to have a piece of cloth. The outer garment was seamless, we are told. It may have been a gift from his mother or perhaps even of the women who ministered to his needs in Galilee (Lk 8:1f.). In Catholic symbolism the seamless robe became the image of the unity of the church, but that is reading something into the text that isn't there.

The dividing of the clothes of Jesus underscores the utter callousness of the soldiers in carrying out their gruesome task. The booty belongs to the victors. But it also speaks of the abject poverty of Jesus. He dies without a shirt on his back, as we might say. But by his poverty millions of Jesus' followers have become spiritually rich.

C. The Time (v. 25). "And it was the third hour when they crucified him."

Mark divides the day of Jesus' death into three-hour periods. The crucifixion took place on the third hour, i.e., 9 o'clock in the morning. In verse 33 we are told that darkness came over the land on the sixth hour. Then in verse 34 Mark tells us that Jesus uttered his death-cry at the ninth hour. Besides these three references, we have already been told that the Jewish authorities brought Jesus to Pilate early in the morning (v.1), and in verse 42 it is stated that they took his body down in the evening. There we have five references to time. That is most unusual, but then there is no day in the Gospel records that comes close to the significance that Good Friday holds. It almost seems as if Mark is giving us a countdown of an extremely important event—9 AM, 12 PM, 3 PM, and then: death.

John's Gospel creates a problem for us, for there we are told that at noon, i.e., the sixth hour, Jesus was still standing before Pilate (19:14). It is difficult to harmonize these chronologies. Since the letters of the alphabet were used for numbers in those days, it may be that the Greek ***gamma*** (the 3rd letter of the alphabet, indicating the third hour) became a double gamma (i.e., six) in the process of copying this account.

The two can hardly be distinguished. We are, of course, dealing with Jewish hours of the day, and so the third hour, when our Lord was crucified, was 9 AM. Matthew and Luke do not give us the time of the crucifixion, and so we are dependent on Mark.

D. The Inscription (v. 26). "The inscription of the charge against him read, 'The King of the Jews'."

If crucifixion was to deter crime, it was useful to have the crime of the condemned person publicized. The practice was, to whiten a board with chalk and to write on it with black or red letters, indicating what crime the victim had committed. Sometimes this plaque was carried before the condemned, as he went to his place of crucifixion. Luke tells us that the inscription was placed "over him" (23:38), so that all who passed by could read it.

Mark gives the inscription in its briefest form. In John's Gospel it is: "Jesus of Nazareth, the King of the Jews." These words in Latin have given us the acronym INRI, which often appears in Christian art. Also, in John's Gospel that title became an occasion for controversy, when the Jewish leaders wanted Pilate to change it to: "He said that he was the king of the Jews." But by then Pilate must have had enough and he refused to have it changed. Moreover, John tells us, that this inscription was written in Greek, Latin and Hebrew. Greek was the language of the world; Latin the language of government; Hebrew the language of the Jewish sacred scriptures. Jesus' death has cosmic significance

Although Jewish bystanders made fun of this title, it proclaims for all times that Jesus is indeed a king, although his kingdom is not of this world. There is an old Latin version of a psalm, quoted by Justin Martyr in his Dialogue With Trypho the Jew, who had argued that the cross was not referred to in the OT: "the Lord reigns from the tree." He does indeed!

"King of my life, I crown Thee now, Thine shall the glory be. Lest I forget Thy thorn crowned brow, Lead me to Calvary."

Chapter 10

Christ's Death on the Cross Mark 15:27-41

On the day that our Lord was crucified, two criminals were crucified with him. Mark reports, "And with him they crucified two bandits, one on his right and one on his left" (v. 26). Luke calls them evil doers, translated by the KJV as "malefactors" under the influence of a Latin compound noun, meaning "evil doers." Matthew and Mark call them bandits, robbers, brigands, thieves.

In an Old Latin text they are given the names: Zoathan and Camma. In an apocryphal book, the Acts of Pilate they are called Dysmas and Gestas. The Gospels do not give their names.

Some Bible students have suggested that there was going to be a crucifixion on that particular day anyway, and that Jesus was crucified in the place of the bandit and murderer, Barabbas. The mention of these two bandits, one to the right and one to the left, was reported by the Evangelists, perhaps, to underscore the indignity to which the innocent Jesus was subjected.

Luke saw this association of the two criminals with Jesus in his death as a fulfilment of Isaiah 53:12, where it is said, "He was numbered with the transgressors" (Lk 22:37). A copyist later carried this saying from Luke over into Mark, and so some of the older English Bibles have an extra verse at this point (v. 28). But the better manuscripts do not have this quotation in Mark, and the NIV and other versions go directly from verse 27 to verse 29.

Mark omits entirely the dialogue between Jesus and the penitent evildoer, who acknowledged his guilt and to whom our Lord opened the gates of paradise. To begin with, however, these two bandits had also reviled Jesus, and that leads us to the threefold mockery recorded by Mark.

I. THE THREEFOLD MOCKERY

A. By the Passersby (vv. 29,30). "Those who passed by derided him, shaking their heads and saying, 'Aha! You who would destroy the temple and build it in three days, save yourself, and come down from the cross'."

Mark has a predilection for a threefold pattern: Jesus prays three times in Gethsemane; Peter denies Jesus three times; the account of Jesus' crucifixion is divided into three three-hour periods; and now we have a threefold mockery.

First the passersby mock Jesus. They are not identified further, but they can hardly be any other than common Jewish people. Mark says quite literally that they "blasphemed" Jesus. Jesus had been accused of blasphemy at the beginning of his ministry (Mk 2:6,7), when he forgave sins. And, at the end of his life, as he stood before the Sanhedrin, he was again accused of blasphemy, because he claimed to be Messiah. Now he hangs on the cross, and the passersby blaspheme him. The word "blaspheme" is used here in a rather general sense, meaning to insult, to mock. According to its etymology, the word means simply to say something bad about someone.

They mock Jesus not only with what they say, but with their body language. They wag their heads in derision. This gesture is well known already in Old Testament times. The suffering Psalmist complains, "They make mouths at me; they shake their heads" (22:7). And in Lamentations 2:14 it is said of the victorious enemies who destroyed Jerusalem, "All who pass by clap their hands at you; they hiss and wag their heads at the daughter of Jerusalem." That language is reflected in our text. To wag one's head is to express disgust.

"Aha" they say, "the one who destroys the temple and builds it up in three days." That echoes the charge made by false witnesses at Jesus' trial. How did these passersby know about that charge? Perhaps by now the report of Jesus' cleansing of the temple just before Passover had spread all over Jerusalem, and people interpreted that symbolical action to mean that Jesus was out to destroy the temple. But Jesus had never said that he would destroy the Jerusalem temple. When he first cleansed the temple, at the beginning of his ministry, he said, "Destroy this temple, and in three days, I will raise it up" (Jo 2:19). For his readers, John the Evangelist explains, that he was talking about the temple of his body (v. 21).

The destruction of the temple, Christ's body, was in fact going on at that very moment before the eyes of the passersby, but they were too blind to see that. But in three days he would rise from the grave, and this miraculous event would be the historical foundation for the building of the church, also called the body of Christ.

The bypassers also challenge Jesus, to save himself by coming down from the cross. No doubt they had heard or even witnessed some of Christ's mighty deeds. Now they challenge him to do one more: come down from the cross. But by not saving himself, Jesus was doing the greatest miracle of all times: saving humanity from sin and the power of death.

B. The Jewish Hierarchy (vv. 31,32a). "In the same way the chief priests, along with the scribes, were also mocking him among themselves, saying, 'He saved others; he cannot save himself. Let the Messiah, the King of Israel come down from the cross now, so that we may see and believe'."

It is somewhat surprising to find members of the Sanhedrin among the bystanders and mockers. One might have thought that the dignity of their position would have kept them away from the scene of the crucifixion. Their presence indicates how profoundly they hated Jesus. But, instead of addressing their sarcastic remarks at Jesus, they do the jesting among themselves. No doubt they spoke loudly enough for Jesus to hear them, but ostensibly they addressed one another.

The verb to mock (***empaizo***) means to make fun of, to jeer, to ridicule, to sneer. Luke has an even stronger verb; he has, "they turned up their noses at him" (23:35). They say sneeringly, "He saved others; he cannot save himself." In one sense they gave marvellous witness to the words and works of Jesus: He saved others. The word "saved" is used in more than one way in the Gospels. Sometimes it means to heal, at other times to restore to life (e.g., the daughter of Jairus, Mark 5:23), or simply to deliver from some peril. But it is also used to describe the experience of the forgiveness of sins. "Your faith has saved you," said Jesus to the sinful woman (Lk 7:50).

Of course they did not intend to witness to Jesus' saving works; their mockery suggests that they thought of him as a fraud, because he couldn't save himself. They had not heard or, if they had, had not understood what Jesus had taught: "Whoever wishes to save his own life will lose it" (Mk 8:35). It was precisely because he wouldn't save himself and come down from the cross, that he could save others. Had he saved himself he would not have saved those who believe in him from eternal destruction.

The story is told of the Christian Sadhu, Sundar Singh, that he and a companion were travelling through the Himalayas on foot one day. It began to snow heavily and the temperature dropped. Suddenly they came upon a person lying on the path almost frozen to death. Sunder's companion hurried on to save himself from freezing to death, but Sunder lifted the half-dead man up and carried him on his back. That brought back life to the frozen fellow and also warmed up Sunder Singh. As they trudged along they suddenly came upon the body of Sunder's travel companion. He had frozen to death. In his attempt to save his life, he had lost it. Sundar, who was willing to lose his life had saved his own.

The rulers remembered the claim that Jesus had made before the high priest Caiaphas, that he was the Christ, i.e., the Messiah, God's anointed One. And so they mockingly call him that: "The Christ (Messiah) the king of Israel, let him come down from the cross."

In the thinking of the Jews at that time, the Messiah was to establish the throne of David, the kingdom, and so Messiah and king of Israel are used quite synonymously. In the eyes of the Romans, of course, the claim to Messiahship meant nothing. But for someone to claim that he was king of the Jews, was seditious, and that's the question Pilate had asked. Jesus had, of course, explained to Pilate, that his kingdom was not of this world.

They say, if Jesus would come down from the cross, they would "see and believe." But they got the order of these two verbs wrong. It is only when people believe, that their eyes are opened to see, to grasp, to understand what Messiahship is all about. To the doubting Thomas, the risen Christ would say later, "Blessed are those who have not seen and yet have come to believe."

But there was a third party that mocked Jesus.

C. The Dying Bandits (v. 32b). "Those who were crucified with him also taunted him."

Mark uses different words for the mockery of each of the three groups. The passersby "blaspheme" (***blasphemeo***) (v. 29), the Jewish hierarchy "ridicules" (***empaizo***) (v. 31), the two bandits "taunt" him (***oneidizo***) (v. 32b). This last verb is in the imperfect and that suggests that they kept on reviling him.

On the cross Jesus has no friends. He is a solitary righteous figure, surrounded on all sides by enemies. But the Jesus whom they vilified, became the Savior of one of these two wretched men. One of them acknowledged his guilt and received the assurance of a place in Christ's kingdom. Mark omits this detail, as well as the reference to the mocking of the soldiers (Lk 23:36-43). Jesus, who refused to save himself, saved one of the two bandits in the hour of his death. This has often been a comfort to those who have prayed for many years for the salvation of a loved one, hoping that before they breathe their last, they will put their faith in Christ, However, the fact that one of the bandits was saved in the hour of his death, should not be an encouragement to postpone getting right with God until life's final hour.

II. THE SUFFERING OF DEATH

A. The Darkness at Noon (v. 33). "When it was noon, darkness came over the whole land until three in the afternoon."

Between the crucifixion which took place at nine o'clock in the morning and the sixth hour, i.e., noon, we have the mockery of the various groups gathered at the cross. No one showed mercy to God's Son. Now it is high noon, and nature puts on mourners' clothing; darkness covers the land.

One is reminded of the darkness that came over the land of Egypt for three days in the days of Moses. Also, when God through his prophet predicted punishment on Jerusalem, he said, "Her sun sets at midday; she is shamed and disgraced" (Jer 15:9). Predictions of the day of the Lord repeatedly contain the grim prospect of darkness at noonday. Amos says, "On that day, says the Lord God, the sun shall set at midday, and the light shall be darkened on earth in the daytime" (8:9,10). These passages speak of the sun losing its light at midday, at the sixth hour.

The darkness that came over the land when Jesus was crucified has been understood in different ways:

(a) Either as a natural phenomenon, such as an eclipse, a dust storm, a locust plague;

(b) or as a figurative description, reflecting Old Testament language of divine judgment.

However we explain this darkness, it was a sign of divine judgment. It was also a sign of nature's sadness when the Maker of this world died. Some readers have even suggested that it was the external aspect of what went on internally in Christ's soul, for in the midst of this cosmic darkness he cries out, "My God, my God, why have you forsaken me," known as the cry of dereliction, of God-forsakenness. The place of eternal punishment is often described as outer darkness. Our Lord suffered eternal punishment in our place and stead.

B. The Cry of Dereliction (v. 34). "At three o'clock Jesus cried out with a loud voice, '*Eloi Eloi lema sabachthani*?' which means, 'My God, my God, why have you forsaken me?'"

Jesus has been abandoned by his disciples, nailed to a cross by Roman soldiers, mocked by the religious hierarchy as well as by wretched criminals. Darkness covers the land. There is nothing, absolutely nothing to indicate that God was on Jesus' side in this dreadful hour. And so, out of the depths of this dereliction there comes the cry, "My God, My God, why have you forsaken me?" These are the opening words of Psalm 22.

As Jesus faced the agony of death, according to Mark's Gospel, Jesus resorted to his Aramaic mother tongue in quoting Psalm 22 (He addresses God as Eloi). Nowhere prior to this occasion is it recorded that Jesus used the address "my God" in his prayers. He always prayed to his Father. However, this was not a cry of despair; Jesus is after all calling on "his" God.

The cry of dereliction has been hard for Bible readers to accept.

(a) Some have thought Jesus quoted the entire Psalm, which ends with a very confident note: "To him, indeed, shall all who sleep in the earth bow down, before him shall bow all who go down to the dust; and they shall live" (Ps 22:29). According to this reading, Jesus' death cry is really a cry of victory. But that doesn't quite ring true. Why should the Evangelists have quoted only the beginning of the Psalm, not the conclusion, if they did not mean to say that Jesus was forsaken by God?

(b) Another line of thought is that Jesus wasn't forsaken by God at all, but only "felt" forsaken. And there is some truth in this, no doubt. Jesus did not question the existence of God; he didn't doubt God's power; but he was overwhelmed by the silence of God. And yet there seems to be more here than simply the feeling of dereliction. He was, in fact, forsaken.

(c) Some copyists of the NT manuscripts found this saying so hard to understand, that they changed the word "forsaken" to "taunted" (*oneidizo* as in v. 32). But the German professor Schmiedel writes, that "the cry of dereliction is an absolutely trustworthy saying, because no one would have ever put these words into the mouth of Jesus, had he not spoken them."

(d) And so we must humbly accept this cry of Jesus as a statement of God-forsakenness. Jesus was bearing the sins of the world. He was suffering the torments of eternal punishment for all humanity. "For our sake he made him to be sin who knew no sin, so that in him we might become the righteousness of God" (2 Cor 5:21). God was in Christ reconciling the world to himself (2 Cor 5:19). "He himself bore our sins in his body on the cross, so that, free from sins, we might live for righteousness; by his wounds you have been healed" (1 Pet 2:24). Because he was forsaken by God on the cross, no child of God will ever be forsaken. Because he spoke these profoundly poignant words on the cross, you and I will never need to say, "My God, my God, why have you forsaken me."

In Rembrandt's 17th century painting of "The Three Crosses," the Dutch painter pictures the crowds standing around the cross and gazing at the Crucified. Right at the edge of the painting is another figure, almost hidden in the shadows. Art critics say that's Rembrandt's face. He wanted to say in deep contrition, that his sins had also contributed to the Savior's death.

C. The Offering of Wine Vinegar (vv. 35,36). "When some of the bystanders heard it, they said, 'Listen, he is calling for Elijah.' And someone ran, filled a sponge with sour wine, put it on a stick, and gave it to him to drink, saying 'Wait, let us see whether Elijah will come to take him down'"

Evidently the bystanders had inadvertently or perhaps deliberately confused "Eloi" (God) with "Elias" (Elijah). In Jewish tradition Elijah was portrayed as wonder worker, who was to precede the coming of Messiah. The Jewish hierarchy had just mocked Jesus' claim to Messiahship, and so they add to the mockery by suggesting that Elijah might deliver Jesus

In order to keep him alive a little longer, and to give Elijah a chance to take him down from the cross, they offer him a drink called *oxos* in Greek. The word means simply "sharp," and refers to a peasant wine, drunk by Roman soldiers. This act recalls Psalm 69:22, "They gave me gall for my bread, and for my thirst they gave me vinegar to drink." Because Jesus was lifted up, they needed a reed on which they affixed a sponge with sour wine, and gave him to drink. Others shouted that they should wait a little longer, just to see whether Elijah would come and deliver him from the cross.

D. The Death Cry (v. 37). "Then Jesus gave a loud cry and breathed his last."

Crucifixion was particularly gruesome because the victims usually screamed with rage and pain, with curses and outbursts of nameless despair. But in the case of Jesus we have none of that. Luke adds a beautiful prayer, that Jesus prayed, known as a bedtime prayer for Jewish children: "Father, into your hands I commit my spirit." It was a kind of Hebrew equivalent of our, "Now I lay me down to sleep, I pray thee Lord my soul to keep."

Crucified victims often lived in torment for some time, if they were not asphyxiated by hanging on the cross. But our Lord died immediately after his final prayer, and the triumphant shout "it is finished," found in the Gospel of John. He had the power to lay down his life and he had the power to take it again. We shall witness the latter on Easter morning, when Christ rose from the dead, never to die again.

III. BETWEEN DEATH AND BURIAL

A. The Rending of the Veil (v. 38). "And the curtain of the temple was torn in two, from top to bottom."

When Jesus stood before Caiaphas, the high priest, false witnesses accused him of threatening to destroy the temple. And when he hung on the cross passersby mocked him, saying "Aha, the one destroying the temple and building it up in three days." And now the destruction of the temple has begun.

The tearing of the veil in two, from top to bottom, is a way of saying that it was completely torn. The passive voice ("the curtain of the temple was torn in two"), suggests that God was the agent; this was an act of God. Even if it should have been caused by the earthquake, which Matthew mentions in connection with the tearing of the veil (Mt 27:54), it was still an act of God. There has been some debate over which curtain it was that was torn in two. In the Herodian temple there were two major curtains—one between the court of the priests and the holy place, and the other between the holy place and the holy of holies.

One argument in favor of the outer veil is that it would be easily visible by the public. In favor of the inner veil is Hebrews 10:19,20, "Therefore, brothers, since we have confidence to enter the sanctuary by the blood of Jesus, by the new and living way that he opened for us through the curtain (that is, through his flesh)... let us approach with true heart in full assurance of faith."

The tearing of the inner veil would have been visible only to the priests on duty, and some Bible scholars suggest that these priests would have kept silent and would not have publicized this embarrassing event. In the Gospel accounts, however, the tearing of the veil is seen as just one of several unusual happenings of which the public became aware. For the Evangelists and their readers the significance of the tearing of the veil was what really mattered.

With the tearing of the curtain, God was indirectly saying that there was no longer a true sanctuary in the Jerusalem temple. Also, the tearing of the veil was a portent of the total destruction that would overtake the temple forty years down the road. The failure on the part of Judaism to recognize Jesus as Messiah, sealed the doom of the temple. The apocryphal Gospel of Peter reports, that when the veil was torn, the Jewish leaders began to lament, "Woe for our sins; the judgment and the end of the Jerusalem has drawn near."

The tearing of the veil also signified, in the light of Hebrews 10:19,20, that all men and women now have free access to God through the blood of Jesus. This means that God's presence is no longer bound to a sanctuary, a holy place, a temple, a cathedral, a church building, but that believers all over the world can approach God in their homes, on the field, in school, in the factory. Prior to the 16th century Reformation, the Waldenses were persecuted for, among other reasons, worshiping in barns. It was an overwhelming experience for Martin Luther, after years of monastic life, trying to find a gracious God, to discover that he could come boldly into the presence of God simply in the name of Jesus. He did not need the mediation of priests; he didn't need to come through Mary; but he could approach the throne of grace by the blood of Jesus. The curtain was torn, and the way to God was open.

B. The Reaction of the Bystanders (w. 39-41).

1. The Centurion (v.39). "Now when the centurion, who stood facing him, saw that in this way he breathed his last, he said, 'Truly this man was God's Son'."

The centurion, presumably one of the four soldiers, was deeply moved by what he had witnessed. This man had no doubt seen many other people die, but never had he witnessed a death such as this. Mark says, "When the centurion saw." What did he see? No doubt he had seen the darkness at noonday; he had seen how people around the cross mocked and taunted Jesus. No doubt he also heard what Jesus said when he hung between earth and sky, and, finally, he saw Jesus give up his spirit. And so he breaks out in his confession: "Truly this man was God's Son."

Several English versions render the word "son" with small "S." The reason for that is, that a pagan soldier would not have known that Jesus was the unique Son of God. He would have recognized that Jesus was a good and holy man, a divine hero worthy of worship. Such people were often called "sons of god" in the ancient world. We do not know how deeply the centurion had grasped the divinity of Jesus, however, when Mark wrote his Gospel in the sixties, both he and the readers undoubtedly understood this testimony of the centurion to mean that Christ was divine. When Jesus stood before Caiaphas he was asked, "Are you the Son of the Blessed One" (i.e. God)? And Jesus responded, "I am." Now it seems as if the pagan soldier says loud and clear, "He is indeed the Son of God."

Peter, a follower of Jesus, had said, "I don't know this man." The centurion, using the same designation, confesses "this man" is truly the Son of God. Yes, he is both man and God, human and divine. And because he is both, he is able to bring us back to God.

2. The Women (vv. 40,41). "There were also women looking on from a distance; among them were Mary Magdalene, and Mary the mother of James the younger and of Joses, and Salome. These used to follow him and provided for him when he was in Galilee; and there were many other women who had come up with him to Jerusalem."

Although these women say nothing in Mark's account, they are silent witnesses to the death of Jesus. They were so important that Mark mentions them by name. Whereas the disciples of

Jesus had fled and were in hiding for fear of the Jews, these women had gone all the way to Calvary with Jesus. One should, of course, take into account, that the Jewish authorities would not have paid much attention to them, for women were considered of no account in their eyes as witnesses.

However, in the eyes of the Gospel writers, they are important witnesses. The men, who were to be witness of Jesus' passion, had disappeared from the scene, and the women now take their place. Women could not be witnesses in Jewish trials, but here everything is reversed and, as we shall see, they were also the first witnesses of the resurrection. Nowhere in Mark's Gospel, prior to this, are we told that Galilean women had accompanied Jesus or had ministered to his needs, but Luke does give us this information (Lk 8: 1f.). Here, however, the circle is widened. Mark says, "many others had come with him to Jerusalem." And with that Mark ends the story of Christ's passion We are now ready to witness the burial and the resurrection.

J. B. Phillips, of Bible translation fame, writes, "After reading hundreds of volumes on Christ's death, I cannot claim to be much closer to understanding so perilous and costly a mystery. The more I think of it and the more I allow my imagination to fill in the gaps in the terse Gospel narratives, the less I am surprised that from the 6th hour there was darkness over all the land unto the 9th hour. God only knows what fearful battles were being fought, or what agonies were silently endured in that time. All I am certain of is this: the ordeal was endured, the battle won, and through Christ we are free men who can approach the Father with confidence."

Chapter 11

The Burial and Resurrection of Jesus
Mark 15:42-16:8

In Paul's summary of the Christian gospel, found in I Corinthians 15:3,4, he mentions the death, the burial and the resurrection of Jesus as constituting the fundamental historical events on which the Christian faith rests. He writes, "For I handed on to you as of first importance what I in turn had received, that Christ died for our sins in accordance with the scriptures, and that he was buried, and that he was raised on the third day in accordance with the scriptures."

The burial of Jesus is mentioned specifically to verify the reality of his death. It emphasizes the fact that the dead body was laid in the grave, so that the resurrection that followed would be recognized as an objective reality, not as something that Jesus' followers dreamt of or wished so badly, that they convinced themselves that he was indeed alive.

The Gospel writers make special mention in their accounts of the resurrection, that those who visited Jesus' tomb on Easter Sunday morning, did not find his body there. The tomb was empty, although no New Testament writer says that explicitly. Critics have often doubted the fact that the tomb was empty. The French sceptic, Renan, said sarcastically, "You Christians live from the fragrance of the empty tomb." Indeed we do. Did we not have an empty tomb, we would not have a risen Christ.

Tomb veneration was common in ancient Israel. People worshiped at the tomb of prophets (Mt 23:29,30). In fact even today Jews worship at the tomb of David in Jerusalem. But there is no record of Christians ever worshiping at the tomb of Jesus. And there was good reason for that: the body of Jesus was not there. He had risen from the dead.

Today we want to follow the account in Mark's Gospel of Christ's burial and his glorious resurrection.

I. THE BURIAL OF JESUS

A. The Time (v.42). "When evening had come, and since it was the preparation, that is, the day before the Sabbath...."

It was now Friday evening. The days of the week had no names in ancient Israel, with the exception of the 7th day, the Sabbath. But since the Sabbath was the climax of the entire week, the day before the Sabbath was called "Preparation" (*paraskeue* in Greek). The other days were simply numbered. Our Sunday was the first day of the week, Monday the second, and so forth. Mark has Gentile Christians in mind, and it is for their sake that he offers this explanation, for every Jew would know that the day before the Sabbath was the day of preparation.

It was common Roman practice to leave crucified criminals hang on their crosses until wild beasts and vultures had done their gruesome work. The Jews thought that practice to be an abomination, and always removed the bodies of criminals and buried them. Not, however, in private or family graves, but in common graves! In other words, they were not given an honorable burial.

Also, they did not permit the bodies of those punished by hanging, to remain on the stake during Sabbath. And so on the Friday on which Jesus died, sometime in the late afternoon, when the Sabbath began, Jesus' body and those of the other two criminals, had to be removed. And that brings Joseph of Arimathea upon the scene.

B. Joseph the Arimathean (vv. 43-45). "Joseph of Arimathea, a respected member of the council, who was also himself waiting expectantly for the kingdom of God, went boldly to Pilate and asked for the body of Jesus. Then Pilate wondered if he were already dead; and summoning the centurion, he asked him whether he had been dead for some time. When he learned from the centurion that he was dead, he granted the body of Joseph."

This is the first time this Joseph is mentioned. He came from Arimathea, which was in Judea (Lk 3:51), although the precise location of the town is not known. Whether he now lived in Jerusalem or not is not certain either. That he had a private tomb in the city, does not necessarily mean that he lived there, for even some Jews who lived in the Diaspora, had burial plots in Jerusalem, for they wanted to be buried there.

Joseph was a respected member of the council, which probably means the Sanhedrin. If so then Joseph obviously had not agreed with the Sanhedrin's verdict. Perhaps he had not even been present during the night when the Sanhedrin condemned our Lord to death.

He was a godly man, awaiting the kingdom of God. Although that expression would be applicable to every devout Jew, Mark seems to suggest that he was a disciple of Jesus. In John's Gospel it is explicitly stated that he was a "secret" disciple (Jo 19:38). Joseph dared to go to Pilate and ask for the body of Jesus. His concern, that Jesus be buried before the Sabbath, overrode his concern, that the body would make him ceremonially unclean. Also, it took courage to ask for the body of a person who had been condemned by a Roman governor for treasonous activity, for he would thereby be identifying with the Jesus movement.

Pilate was surprised to hear that Jesus had already died, and called the centurion to verify the fact that Jesus was dead. According to John's Gospel this was the reason the soldiers did not break the legs of Jesus, in contrast to the other two criminals. Breaking the legs was evidently done to hurry on the death of crucified criminals.

Once Pilate was assured that Jesus was dead, he ordered that the body of Jesus be given to Joseph. For the early church it was probably important to have it confirmed by the highest government authority that Jesus was dead, for later, when the disciples proclaimed the good news of Christ's resurrection from the dead, there were always those sceptics who wondered whether he had actually died.

The last thing the Jewish authorities would have wanted, was that Jesus should be given an honorable burial. Pilate, however, took sweet revenge on the Jews who had forced his hand, and he was quite prepared to hand over the body of Jesus to Joseph, even though he knew this would rankle the Jewish authorities.

C. The Internment (vv. 46,47). "Then Joseph bought a linen cloth, and taking down the body, wrapped it in the linen cloth and laid it in a tomb that had been hewn out of the rock. He then rolled a stone against the door of the tomb. Mary Magdalene and Mary the mother of Joses saw where the body was laid."

Very likely Joseph, who was a man of high standing, had others help him with the purchase of the cloth, the removal of the body, and the burial. No doubt much is left unsaid in this very condensed account. Nothing is said about the washing of the body, the anointing or the use of spices, mentioned in John's Gospel. All that is stated here is, that the body was taken down from the cross and wrapped in fresh linen cloth, just purchased.

The Shroud of Turin first surfaced in 1357, and the debate over its authenticity has continued to this day. But even if it could be proved that it came from the first century, how could one prove that it was Jesus' shroud? Besides, it has no relevance for the good news of the Gospel.

The tomb into which they laid Jesus was hewn out of the rock, a practice well known in those days. Rock quarries often served as suitable sites for such tunnelling. Matthew adds that this particular tomb was Joseph's own tomb (27:60). Sometimes the tunnelling was done horizontally into a wall of rock; at other times vertical shafts were made. From the Gospel accounts it appears as if Joseph's tomb, into which Jesus was laid, had been hewn out of a rock wall, for on Easter Sunday, Peter and John walked right into the tomb. Mark says simply that they rolled a stone over the mouth of the tomb.

Whether we are to think of this stone as a boulder, rolled up to the mouth of the tomb, or a wheel-shaped stone slab that was rolled in a track across the entrance to the tomb, is not quite certain. Many different kinds of tombs have been discovered by archaeologists. The tomb into which Jesus was laid appears to have had an ante-room with a bench, for Mark says (16:5) that a young man sat inside on the right.

Although Mark doesn't mention it, John tells us that Joseph of Arimathea had a companion who participated in the interment process, and that was Nicodemus, a religious leader who had come to Jesus by night (Jo 3:1). He contributed a hundred pounds of spices.

The account of the interment closes with the mention of two Marys. Both of them were already mentioned earlier (v.40), as two of the women who watched from a distance and witnessed the death of Jesus. One of the women, Mary Magdalene, had been delivered from demon possession, and in deep gratitude devoted herself to serve the Lord. Her birthplace was Magdala, a village on the western shore of the Sea of Galilee. In John's Gospel two other Marys are mentioned (Mary, the mother of Jesus and Mary, the wife of Clopas, John 19:25), but Mark mentions only two: Mary Magdalene, and Mary; the mother of Joses. In verse 40 she is said to be also the mother of James the younger, and that is repeated in Mark 16:1. All these women suffered in silent pain as they witnessed the death of their Lord.

Formally the Passion Narrative comes to an end with the burial of Jesus. But no one would ever have written up the passion story if there had not been a joyous and triumphant sequel, namely, the resurrection of Jesus on the first day of the week. And so we would be remiss, if we stopped our study with the burial of Jesus. We move then from what came to be known as Good Friday to Easter Sunday.

II. THE RESURRECTION OF OUR LORD

A. The Visit to the Tomb (16:1,2) "When the Sabbath was over, Mary Magdalene, and Mary the mother of James, and Salome bought spices, so that they might go and anoint him. And very early on the first day of the week, when the sun had risen, they went to the tomb."

These faithful women, disciples of Jesus, must have endured the forced inactivity of the Sabbath day with some agony and impatience. But now that the Sabbath is over, they are no longer merely observers; they are active participants. It is of considerable significance that these women were the first witnesses to the resurrection of Jesus. And since all evidence, according to the Old Testament, rested on two or three witnesses, Mark mentions three women by name. The two Marys had already been named (15:47) as well as Salome (15:40). She was the mother of the sons of Zebedee (Mt 27:56).

The Sabbath came to an end about 6 PM on Saturday, and these women then went and purchased aromatic oils. This was not for mummification of the body, which was an Egyptian practice, but to offset the odors of decomposition. Archaeologists have found perfume bottles, ointment jars and other vessels in ancient Palestinian tombs.

These women did not anticipate a resurrection. If they had ever heard Jesus say, that he would rise from the dead on the third day, they weren't conscious of that prediction. As far as they were concerned, Jesus was dead, and so they prepare to anoint his body. This was an act of deep devotion, an expression of their love and loyalty to Jesus.

Very early on the first day of the week, at sunrise, they are on their way to the tomb. The first day of the week later became the day on which Christ's followers gathered to worship the risen Lord. This is mentioned twice in the New Testament (Acts 20:7 and 1 Cor 16:1). And because Christ, by his resurrection, was declared to be Lord, the first day of the week came also to be called "the Lord's day" (Rev 1:10).

Bible readers have often wondered how we get three days and three nights out of the chronology of the Synoptic Gospels, and so there have been attempts to place the death of Christ not on Friday, but on Thursday. Evidence for this view is sometimes sought in John's Gospel, where we seem to have a somewhat different chronology. That, however, is not the majority opinion. Since part of a day was counted as a day, the three days that Jesus was in the grave, would be Friday, Saturday and Sunday. That allows for only two nights, but "three days and three nights" is idiomatically the same as when it is said that Christ rose "on the third day."

B. The Stone Before the Tomb (vv. 3,4). "They had been saying to one another, 'Who will roll away the stone for us from the entrance to the tomb?' when they looked up, they saw that the stone, which was very large, had already been rolled back."

Rolling a flat stone in front of the mouth of the tomb was relatively easy, once it had slipped into the groove cut in the bedrock. To roll it back, however, was a different matter. On the way to the tomb, then, it occurred to these women, that without help they wouldn't be able to enter the tomb. "Who will roll away the stone for us," they ask each other. And that question would apply, whether it was a boulder or a flat stone resembling a wheel.

Mark says nothing about the sealing of the tomb or the posting of a guard. Only Matthew gives us this information. What is so ironical is, that the Jewish leaders, who so often accused Jesus of breaking the Sabbath, when he healed people or did some other good deed, violated the Sabbath themselves by going to Pilate on the day after the preparation, i.e., on the Sabbath (Mt 26:62), to request a guard, for fear that Jesus' disciples might come and steal the body. They must have heard somewhere that Jesus had spoken about rising on the third day, for they ask Pilate for a guard up to the third day.

Evidently the women knew nothing about all that. They had watched as Jesus' body was laid in the tomb and the mouth of the tomb was closed with a stone. Mark underscores the problem of removing the stone by adding, "And the stone was very big." In a famous fifth century Greek manuscript (Codex Bezae) there is an interesting addition in the Gospel of Luke: "Twenty men could not roll it away."

But as these women looked up, they saw, to their great surprise, that the stone had been rolled away. Mark makes no attempt to explain how this had happened. Matthew adds that there was a great earthquake and an angel of the Lord, descending from heaven, came and rolled back the stone (28:2). Since the stone was rolled away and the mouth of the tomb was open, the women went into the ante-chamber of the tomb. The body of Jesus was gone. An empty tomb by itself was, of course, not a proof of a resurrection, and the women may have begun to speculate on who had removed the body of Jesus. But they are about to get an answer, for, as they enter the tomb, they see a young man sitting on the right side, arrayed in a white robe; and they were amazed.

C. The Vision of the Young Man in White (vv. 5-7).

I. The Amazement (v. 5). "As they entered the tomb, they saw a young man, dressed in a white robe, sitting on the right side; and they were alarmed."

To see a person in the tomb would by itself have been enough to frighten any one. But this young man was brilliantly clothed. Matthew calls him an angel and no doubt that is also what Mark meant, for this young man speaks here as God's messenger who reveals to these women the great mystery of what has happened.

In the color symbolism of the New Testament white is primarily the color of heaven. This can be seen most clearly in the book of Revelation. Those who go home to glory, for example, are all clothed in white (Rev 7:13). And when Jesus comes in glory, his attendants are all clothed in white (Rev 19:14). When Jesus was on the Mount of Transfiguration, his clothes became dazzling white (Mk 9:3). God's messenger, who had come to inform these women that Jesus had risen from the dead, reflects the glory of heaven.

The response of the women to the presence of a heavenly messenger is that of amazement — always the proper response when God makes himself known. Mark uses an unusually strong compound verb for "amazement" (*ekthambeomai*). It includes an element of dread and terror and surprise. Mark's Gospel is known for its emphasis on amazement.

2. The Announcement (v. 6). "But he said to them, 'Do not be alarmed; you are looking for Jesus of Nazareth, who was crucified. He has been raised, he is not here. Look, there is the place they laid him'."

There are considerable differences in the details of the resurrection story in our Gospels but, as A. M. Hunter of Aberdeen points out, if all these stories could be woven into a perfect harmony without discrepancies, we might well be suspicious of their trustworthiness. Discrepancies need not be viewed as contradictions, but as authentic reporting from different vantage points.

As so often in the Scriptures, when human beings shrink in terror in the presence of a revelation of God, the angel here also calms their fears. Don't be alarmed; don't be terrified; don't be amazed. And to calm their fears, he assures them that he knows why they have come. You are seeking Jesus and, since that name was common enough, he makes sure there is no misunderstanding: it is Jesus of Nazareth. And if that should still leave the question open, he adds: "the one crucified." So they know that they are at the right tomb. (Critics, who deny the resurrection, have at times suggested that the women went to the wrong tomb.)

And then comes the grand surprise: "He is risen; he is not here; look at the place where they laid him." That the tomb was empty, they could see for themselves, but that could be explained in any number of ways. For example, the enemies of Jesus later spread the rumor that the disciples had stolen the body. However, the heavenly messenger gives them a word of revelation: "He is risen." The verb is in the passive voice, meaning that God raised him. So God had reversed the judgment of the Sanhedrin and of Pilate. All those who had mocked Jesus, as he suffered on the cross, were put to shame. He was alive. And that meant that all his wonderful teachings and mighty deeds were authenticated; they were believable. He was the Messiah they had taken him to be.

3. The Commission (v. 7). "But go, tell his disciples and Peter that he is going ahead of you to Galilee; there you will see him, just as he told you."

After assuring the women that Jesus was alive, the angel commands them to let his disciples know that he will meet them in Galilee. Although the disciples had forsaken him in his hour of trial, and although Peter had denied him three times, they are still called "his disciples," and that is a comfort also for us who often deny Jesus as our Lord by our many failures.

What is particularly touching about this commission is, that they are to tell Peter. He has not been mentioned since his denial, but there is forgiveness even for one who so shamefully distanced himself from his Lord. He too is to go to Galilee, where his Lord will meet him. We all know about that emotionally charged meeting by the lakeside, as our Lord restored his fallen disciples and called him to be a shepherd of Christ's flock (Jo 21:15-19).

The meeting in Galilee had been predicted by Jesus even before his suffering and death (Mk 14:28). The verb "to go ahead" (***proago***) suggests that he is the Shepherd who leads the flock. When the Shepherd was smitten, the flock was scattered, but now he will gather his flock once more. "There you will see him just as he told you." Other Gospels fill in what Mark omits here: the many appearances of the risen Lord in Jerusalem and also in Galilee. Paul rounds off these accounts by mentioning Christ's appearances to his brother James, and also his appearance to 500 people on one occasion. All of these were witnesses to Christ's victory over sin and death.

D. The Fear of the Women (v. 8). "So they went out and fled from the tomb, for terror and amazement had seized them; and they said nothing to anyone, for they were afraid."

Their flight from the empty tomb was not like the flight of the disciples when Jesus was captured. They fled to save their skins; these women fled because they were overwhelmed by the presence and action of God. Their fear was similar to that of Peter, James and John, who saw Christ transformed on the Mount of Transfiguration. Mark says of them, "they were exceedingly afraid" (9:6).

Confronted with God's mysterious action, these women didn't really know how to respond. They just couldn't comprehend the wonder of it all. They had never experienced anything like it. As devout Jews they may have wondered whether Christ's resurrection marked the beginning of the last day, when all the dead would rise.

When it is said that they told no one, that doesn't mean that they failed to carry out the commission given to them by the angel, namely, to tell his disciples. The Emmaus disciples later say, "Some women of our group astounded us. They were at the tomb early this morning and when they did not find the body there they came back and told us that he was alive (Lk 24:22). Rather, in the presence of God's mysterious act, they lapsed into deep silence.

In the better manuscripts of Mark, his Gospel ends with verse 8, "And they were afraid." And because that ending seems so abrupt, some scholars hold that the original ending was lost. In any case, we now have two or three other endings in some manuscripts and some ancient versions. But the present ending is thoroughly consistent with the motifs of astonishment and fear that can be traced throughout the Gospel. The account of the empty tomb was soul-shaking, and Mark, so it seems, ends his Gospel with the emphasis on amazement, awe and wonder. The resurrection cannot be understood or explained. It can only be believed and proclaimed.

Without the resurrection of Jesus there would be no church. Had the cross been the end of the story, Jesus' followers would have despaired, and they never would have thought of writing the Passion Narrative. If Christ had not risen, there would be no New Testament. Who would have taken the trouble to write the story of a man who had made tremendous claims to deity, but whose career ended in a shameful death? And that is true not only of the Gospels, but of all the letters of the New Testament as well, for they are shot through with rays from the resurrection sun.

The fact that the Christian church from its earliest days began to meet on Sunday to worship Christ as Lord, instead of on the Jewish Sabbath, is powerful testimony to the reality of the resurrection in the lives of the early Christians. Also, from the earliest days of the church the believers celebrated the Lord's Supper with great joy, for they believed that the risen Christ was in their midst when they ate the bread and shared the cup.

And by now, for almost two millennia, Christ's followers have witnessed to the presence of the risen Christ in their lives; they have faced death with confidence, knowing that the one who raised Jesus from the dead would also raise them out of death on the great resurrection morning, when the trumpet will sound and the dead will be raised incorruptible.

Other Books by David Ewert

How the Bible Came to Us
Stalwart for the Truth
Die Wunderwege Gottes mit der Gemeinde
And Then Comes the End
The Holy Spirit in the New Testament
From Ancient Tablets to Modern Translations
The Church in a Pagan Society
Proclaim Salvation
A Journey of Faith
When the Church Was Young
A Testament of Joy
The Church Under Fire
Honor These People
Ist das Heil verlierbar?
Der Heilige Geist—Sein Wesen und Wirken
Verstehst Du Was Du Liest?
How to Understand the Bible
Finding Our Way
Searching the Scriptures
Emmanuel: God With Us

ABOUT THE AUTHOR

David Ewert has been involved in the teaching and preaching ministry at home and abroad since 1944. After attending several Bible training schools, he earned degrees from The University of British Columbia (B.A.), Wheaton Graduate School (M.A.), Central Baptist Seminary, Toronto (B.D.), Luther Seminary (M.Th.), and McGill University, Montreal (Ph.D.)

He was awarded an honorary doctorate by the Mennonite Brethren Biblical Seminary, Fresno, California. David is the author of numerous articles and books in the field of biblical studies. He and his wife are the parents of five children, twelve grandchildren, and two great-grandchildren. David and Lena presently make their home in Abbotsford, BC. They are members of the Bakerview Mennonite Brethren Church.